COLLINS

CAMCORDER
Questions & Answers

COLLINS

CAMCORDER
Questions & Answers

Your Key to Successful Home Videos

STEVE PARKER

ABOUT THE AUTHOR

Steve Parker is a journalist, author and photographer working predominantly in the consumer electronics field. He was involved with the TV series *Shoot the Video* and *I, Camcorder*, and has written extensively for video magazines, including *Video Camera*, *What Video*, *Camcorder User* and *What Camcorder*, and the part-works *CameraWise* and *Camcorder KnowHow*. He is the author of *Photographing Babies and Children* (1994) and *Collins Camcorder Handbook* (1993), both published by HarperCollins.

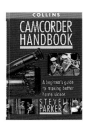

First published in 1995 by
HarperCollins Publishers, London

Illustrations: Rt Illustrators

Edited, designed and typeset by Haldane Mason, London

A catalogue record book for this book is available from the British Library.

ISBN 0 00 412734 X

Printed and bound in Italy

Photographic Acknowledgements
All photographs by the author except: 10 (bottom), 86 (bottom left), Mike Parker; 25 (bottom), Shona Wood; 15 (top), 76 (top), Panasonic UK; 18, 76 (bottom), 98, Sony UK; 52, Sharp UK; 57 (right), Apex Ltd; 60 (bottom), CZ Scientific; 65, Fuji UK; 66 (top), Matsushita Japan; 67 (top), Drytech Ltd; 108, VideoTech Design; 11, 101, 131 (bottom), Canon UK.

CONTENTS

2 ACCESSORIES AND SOUND • 54

3 EDITING YOUR VIDEOS • 74

INTRODUCTION

Why are shutter speeds high and lux levels low? Why should your balance be white but your tapes be blacked? How can manufacturers produce camcorders that are only 8mm? And why do you need to know if your TV is a PAL or not?

Video can seem a daunting hobby to the beginner. Even plugging your camcorder into your TV can resemble a horror movie – or a spaghetti western. The situation is not helped by the fact that manufacturers enjoy selling systems that are incompatible with each other, and it is difficult to know where to go to get a straight answer on even the simplest subject.

Problem areas

Collins Camcorder Questions & Answers tackles each of the potential problem areas in video in a straightforward and logical order – because video does have a certain logic to it. Most of the buttons on a camcorder serve a useful purpose, and the different plugs and wires do have a reason for being there.

In the pages that follow, over 300 of the most important questions in video are posed and answered. Accompanying the answers are over 200 full colour photographs and diagrams that illustrate and illuminate the written explanations. The questions are conveniently divided into different topics, and each spread deals with a specific area. Each topic begins with a question that explains the basics of the subject, and further questions address the more complex areas, which advanced users will find useful. An easy-reference glossary at the back provides at-a-glance explanations of the important technical terms.

From recording to editing

The book is divided into three main sections. The first deals with how the camcorder records an image, beginning with an explanation of how camcorders differ from each other, and dealing, in turn, with the important camcorder functions – such as exposure, white balance and autofocus. Although it is possible to use the camcorder on fully automatic, a quick read of these sections will help you to understand why a camcorder has difficulty recording fireworks without the colours looking washed out, or why a camcorder does not always focus accurately on particular subjects.

Section two looks at sound recording and at accessories – extra pieces of equipment that can dramatically improve the quality of your picture and your sound, which is just as important.

The final section deals with post-production – playing back what you have recorded and tweaking your shots to make them look more interesting and more professional. There is a lot of extra equipment on offer in this area, and *Collins Camcorder Questions & Answers* explains what all the various black boxes available for video post-production do. As well as looking at equipment, this section deals with the art of movie-making. It addresses such questions as how long each shot in your movie should last on-screen and how to plan and produce simple sequences to make your movies more watchable.

Changing pace

There is a danger in writing a definitive guide to a subject that evolves so quickly. At the time of writing, for instance, there are six domestic camcorder formats – VHS, VHS-C, S-VHS, S-VHS-C, 8mm and Hi8. Yet by the time you read this, the pace-setters in the video industry might well have introduced products that use a new digital video format, DVC.

This being said, new development would alter the emphasis of only a tiny proportion of the book. Many of the principles explained here hold as true for old cine cameras as they do for modern camcorders – and they'll still hold true in years to come.

THE CAMCORDER

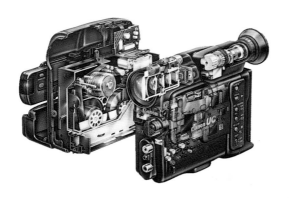

CHOOSING A CAMCORDER

I want to buy a camcorder, but I am confused by the different formats. I have been told that hi-band camcorders are better than lo-band. What is the difference, and will I have to pay more for hi-band?

There are six domestic camcorder formats to choose from, divided into two families – those that use 8mm-wide tape and those that use half-inch tape (the VHS family). VHS camcorders use the same cassettes as VHS video recorders. VHS-C camcorders use VHS tape, but the cassettes are smaller. The 8mm format was designed for camcorders, hence the smaller cassettes. Each of these formats has a more expensive 'hi-band' cousin (Super VHS, S-VHS-C and Hi8 respectively). These use the same size of cassette, but picture quality is better and the recording systems more advanced.

I have read that hi-band camcorders give over 400 lines of resolution, and lo-band formats offer around 240. My TV boasts 625. Will we see camcorders that offer the full 625 lines in the future?

It is a common error to confuse lines of resolution with TV scanning lines. Look closely at your TV screen and you will see it is made up of hundreds of horizontal lines. There are either 625 or 525 lines, depending on your country's TV system. Not all of the lines are used to form the picture – some simply carry information.

Resolution refers to the number of alternate black and white vertical lines per inch that the format can accurately reproduce. The table below shows what the various formats and hardware can resolve.

LCD monitor

lo-band camcorder

portable TV

hi-band camcorder

large-screen TV

| 0 | 100 | 200 | 300 | 400 | 500 | 600 |

FORMAT	PRINCIPAL ADVANTAGES	PRINCIPAL DISADVANTAGES
VHS	Tapes play back in VCRs Long tape-running time	Bulky Limited choice Often expensive
VHS-C	Some models are cheap Tapes play in VCR with adaptor Wide choice Lightweight	Short tape-running time
8mm	Some models are cheap Very wide choice Generally smallest models Even cheapest have good sound	Need leads for playback Short tape-running time
S-VHS	High-quality picture Long tape-running time	Limited choice Bulky Expensive
S-VHS-C	High-quality picture Some are lightweight Relatively wide choice Play in S-VHS VCRs with adaptor	Short tape-running time Most are expensive
Hi8	High-quality picture Wide choice Most are lightweight	Most are expensive Very few Hi8 VCRs

COMPATIBILITY

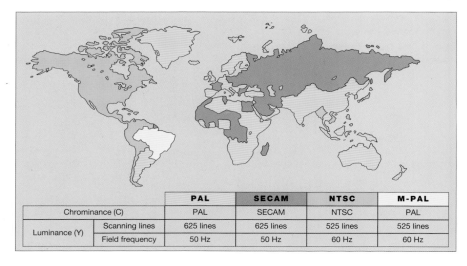

		PAL	SECAM	NTSC	M-PAL
Chrominance (C)		PAL	SECAM	NTSC	PAL
Luminance (Y)	Scanning lines	625 lines	625 lines	525 lines	525 lines
	Field frequency	50 Hz	50 Hz	60 Hz	60 Hz

I have seen cheap camcorders being sold abroad. Are there any disadvantages in buying a camcorder in a foreign country?

You may be tempted by bargains, but buying abroad has its drawbacks. First you have to make sure that the equipment is compatible with your country's TV system. There are three main standards: NTSC (USA, Canada and Japan), PAL (Europe, China and Australia) and SECAM (France, the ex-Soviet States and the Middle East). A more detailed breakdown is given on the above map.

PAL and SECAM pictures are made up of 625 horizontal lines, and NTSC is made up of 525 horizontal lines (see Choosing a Camcorder, p. 12, and Recording an Image, p. 40). PAL and SECAM produce black and white images when played back through the other system, while NTSC is incompatible with the other two. There are also a number of hybrid systems, such as Brazil's PAL-M, which is closer to NTSC than PAL or SECAM. Some VCRs and TVs can play back tapes of a different standard, but most of them are single-standard only.

If you buy equipment abroad, you may have to pay customs charges and sales tax, which could make your apparent bargain as expensive as buying at home.

Can I send camcorder tapes to my relatives who live abroad? I'm worried about the tapes being damaged by X-rays.

 X-rays do not damage tapes, so you can safely send them abroad. Make sure that they are packed firmly and well-insulated with bubble-wrap. If your relatives live in a country with a different TV standard, a video-facilities house can copy and convert your tape. If you have a VHS-C camcorder, you can use a video letter kit (below), which consists of tapes and a cassette adaptor. Send the VHS-C tape and the adaptor, and your relatives can play the tape directly in their VCR.

 **My PAL TV has NTSC playback. When American friends sent me an NTSC tape of their holiday, it played fine, but a copy I made was of dreadful quality. Why is this?**

Many top VCRs can 'read' and play back tapes of a different TV standard, but your PAL VCR outputs a pseudo-NTSC signal, not full NTSC. Most modern TVs can easily cope with such pseudo-signals, because they can scan at 60 frames per second as well as 50 (see Recording an Image, p. 40). VCRs have far less tolerance and record a wobbly picture with poor sound. If you want a copy, you will have to get the tape converted to PAL.

An American NTSC video plays fine in a multi-standard PAL VCR, but it may not copy to another PAL VCR.

CAMCORDER CARE

What lifespan can I expect from my camcorder?

Although it's difficult to generalize, spare parts for products such as camcorders are normally available for at least seven years after the camcorder is launched. The parts that wear out first – the recording heads, motors and mechanical components – should all be capable of at least 1500 hours of use, which is more than adequate.

In general, how reliable are camcorders? Are some faults more common than others?

The most common faults are caused by the users – largely impact damage and contact with liquids, smoke or sand. The most common mechanical fault is dirty video heads, which produces a snowstorm effect. You can clean these yourself with a head cleaner – but avoid buying abrasive types as these can cause wear.

I'm worried about getting sand in my camcorder when I'm on holiday. If I do, will my manufacturer's guarantee cover it?

Guarantees cover only manufacturing and materials defects, but you may be able to extend your household contents insurance to cover accidents. Never put your camcorder on the sand or a towel. When not in use, keep it in a case. Waterproof cases are a good option for the beach.

Be careful when taking your camcorder on the beach – a waterproof housing will keep out sand and surf.

Can bright lights, such as a flash going off, or the sun, damage my camcorder?

At one time, camcorders registered an image using light-sensitive tubes, rather than the CCD imaging chip found in camcorders today. These tubes could easily be blown by bright lights, but CCDs don't suffer from this problem. Flashguns offer no difficulties for the modern camcorder, but the sun can cause other problems, such as backlighting (see Manual Exposure, p. 36) and incorrect white balance (see Lighting Problems, p. 28).

I am thinking of buying a hard case for my camcorder, but am worried about the weight. Are soft cases as effective?

A soft case is perfectly adequate for protecting your camcorder during everyday use. Buy one with movable partitions, so you can fit in all your equipment easily.

POWERING UP

Do batteries wear out? Mine seems to give a lot less running time now than when I first bought it.

Nickel cadmium (NiCad) batteries have a 'chemical memory'. Unless you almost completely discharge them before recharging them, they will give less power next time you use them. Many chargers automatically discharge the battery before recharging to prevent this. If you constantly top them up when there is power in them, 'memory effect' will get worse.

Can a battery be discharged quickly – for example, by attaching it to a car headlamp?

Yes, but it is not recommended. If you fully discharge a NiCad battery, you can reverse its polarity and effectively render it useless. Camcorders and dischargers are designed to cut out before the battery is fully discharged to prevent this.

My battery already suffers from memory effect. Is there any way I can eliminate it, or is it damaged permanently?

Batteries suffering from memory effect are not lost for ever, and can be resurrected. You can gain a bit of life by discharging the battery using a discharger, then fully recharging it. As soon as it is recharged, discharge and recharge it again. If you repeat this discharge/recharge cycle half a dozen times you will begin to see an improvement once you use it on your camcorder. If you salvage your NiCad, don't fall back into bad habits.

NiCad batteries suffer from 'memory effect'– they have to be fully discharged before being recharged. Some camcorders (*right*) use lithium ion batteries, which can be topped up without any problems.

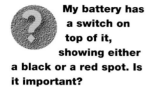 **My battery has a switch on top of it, showing either a black or a red spot. Is it important?**

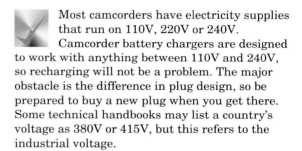 It doesn't actually do anything – it is simply there to remind you whether the battery is charged or not. Flick the switch on your battery from red spot to black when it is flat.

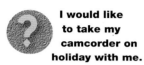 **I would like to take my camcorder on holiday with me. As different countries use different voltages, will I be able to recharge my batteries while I'm away?**

Most camcorders have electricity supplies that run on 110V, 220V or 240V.
Camcorder battery chargers are designed to work with anything between 110V and 240V, so recharging will not be a problem. The major obstacle is the difference in plug design, so be prepared to buy a new plug when you get there. Some technical handbooks may list a country's voltage as 380V or 415V, but this refers to the industrial voltage.

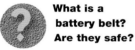 **What is a battery belt? Are they safe?**

Battery belts (below) are extremely useful if you are shooting lengthy events such as weddings, as they give you the running time of several batteries. They are perfectly safe and easy to use.

A STEADY IMAGE

Are some camcorders better at producing a steady image than others?

Some camcorders have one of a number of systems known as 'image stabilization'. The various systems can be split into two broad categories: optical and digital.

The illustrations below show how digital image stabilization works. They represent two consecutive images as they are recorded by the camcorder's CCD, the electronic imaging chip that is the camcorder's equivalent of film in a still camera (see Recording an Image, p. 40). Between the two images, the camcorder has rocked slightly, causing the subject in the second image to be lower in the frame than in the first. With a normal camcorder, this would register as camera shake, but with digital image stabilization, the camcorder doesn't store the whole image. Instead, it enlarges a 70 per cent portion and stores this.

With digital image stablilization, instead of recording the entire image that passes through the lens, only a central portion is transferred to tape.

On the illustrations below, the central 'bold' sections represent this enlarged portion. The camcorder compares each image with the previous one and moves the central portion up and down to keep key elements in the frame in the same position. Compare the inner portions below and you will see that there is no longer any camera shake.

Lower quality

The drawback of digital stabilization systems is that, because they have to enlarge the image, this results in a drop in quality. This does not happen with optical image stabilization systems. Rather than compare consecutive images, optical systems register camcorder movement. They then compensate for it by moving a glass prism inside the lens. This bends the light rays by the right amount to correct for camera shake. As there is no image enlargement, there is no consequent loss of quality.

This central portion moves up and down to compensate for camera shake. Image stabilization can be switched off when the camcorder is mounted on a tripod.

AUTOFOCUS

What does 'autofocus' mean and how does it work?

Autofocus (AF) ensures the camcorder's chosen subject is sharp. It works by shifting the lens elements until light rays from the subject are focused on the image recording chip (CCD). Active systems measure the distance between the camcorder and the subject by sending out one or more infra-red beams. The amount of time it takes the beam to

When I zoom in from wide-angle to telephoto, the image goes blurry momentarily during the zoom. Is there anything I can do about this?

Most camcorders use a passive focusing system. These constantly monitor the image coming through the lens to keep the subject sharp. When you zoom in rapidly, the AF system may not be able to react in time, and the result is a momentary blurring as the system hunts for the correct focus. If you have a camcorder with an external focusing ring, you can avoid this problem by switching to manual focus and prefocusing the lens on the subject.

Accurate focusing is far more critical at the telephoto end than the wide-angle, because the depth of field (the amount of the scene that is sharp in front of and behind the point of focus) is much narrower at the telephoto end (see Depth of Field, p. 38). Because of this, you should first zoom in to the telephoto setting and wait for the AF to focus. Switch to manual focus and zoom out to the wide-angle setting. Start recording, hold the shot for a couple of seconds, then zoom in. Ideally you should use a tripod.

Inner focusing
If your camcorder doesn't have an external focusing ring, it probably uses an internal focus mechanism. In this case, the point of focus will change as you zoom. This doesn't rule out the above method, however, as depth of field may be great enough at the wide-angle setting to render the subject sharp anyway.

hit the subject and bounce back tells the camcorder how far away it is.

Active systems are quick and capable of working in low light. However, they can be fooled by glass and matt black subjects that absorb the light beam. Passive systems analyse the image on the CCD and work on the principle that in-focus subjects have more contrast than blurred subjects. They work well at all distances and lens settings, but they don't work so well in low light or with low-contrast subjects.

When zooming in, passive autofocus systems might hunt for the correct focus, causing momentary blurring and ruining the shot.

You may be able to solve the problem by focusing manually, but question why you want to zoom – cutting from wide shot to close-up will probably have more impact.

MANUAL FOCUS

When should I use manual focus?

Autofocus systems usually ensure a sharp subject, but there are times when manual focus is better. Most AF systems lock on to what is in the centre of the frame; with an off-centre subject they might focus on the background instead. Also, dark subjects offer little contrast for the AF system to lock on to. In both of these situations, manual focus is better.

Some camcorders focus on whatever is in the middle of the frame. If you have deliberately composed a subject that is off-centre, you may find that manual focusing ensures a sharper picture.

Some focusing systems can be fooled when you are shooting through glass, mesh or – as here – bars. It is best to switch to manual focus in this situation.

Contrast-based autofocus systems need a reasonable amount of light to work efficiently. In poor light, manual focus may be your best option – but a wide-angle lens will help to retain sharpness throughout the shot.

The glare of sand, and the lack of contrast it affords, can cause trouble for your focusing system. It may be easier to focus manually, unless you are following a moving subject.

I find it difficult to focus my lens manually. There are no focusing aids in my viewfinder, like there are in my SLR camera, and the viewfinder quality is poor.

Manual focusing can be difficult, especially with colour viewfinders, which lack the quality of black and white ones. Camcorders don't have focusing aids because you are viewing an already-focused TV picture. If the image is too poor to focus properly, your best bet is to use an add-on monitor (see Shooting Accessories, p. 66). These are particularly useful if you have the kind of camcorder that uses an optical viewfinder (no built-in TV, just a square of plastic, like you'd find in a compact camera).

COLOUR AND LIGHT

What is colour temperature?

The colour of light varies with the type of lighting used. To test this, place a lamp by a window during the daytime. Switch on the lamp and look at the difference – the window light looks very blue and the light bulb very yellow. The colour of light is referred to as its colour temperature, and is measured in Kelvin (K). The higher the colour temperature, the cooler, more blue the light. Artificial tungsten lighting is generally taken to be around 3,200K, but in practice, lights can be as low as 2,500K. The table below gives a more detailed breakdown.

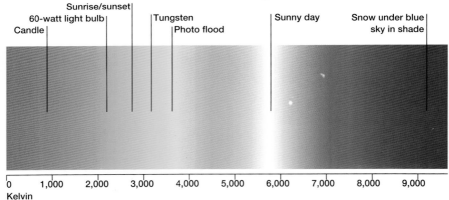

Candle | 60-watt light bulb | Sunrise/sunset | Tungsten / Photo flood | Sunny day | Snow under blue sky in shade

0   1,000   2,000   3,000   4,000   5,000   6,000   7,000   8,000   9,000
Kelvin

What is white balance and how does it work?

Our brain automatically compensates for different colour temperatures, and the camcorder's electronic brain needs similar circuitry. This circuitry is known as white balance or, sometimes, colour balance. The assumption is made that if white objects in the scene are reproduced accurately, all other colours will look right too. Different manufacturers use slightly different systems, but generally they work by comparing the amount of red and blue in a scene. If there is too much blue – say on a very bright day – the camcorder reduces the amount of blue in the signal.

What is the purpose of manual white balance?

Automatic white-balance systems can sometimes be fooled by awkward lighting situations. Some camcorders allow manual control by offering tungsten (3,200K) and daylight (5,600K) pre-sets, and some offer a third setting for fluorescent lighting, which has a range of colour temperature. Some systems also offer white-balance lock. The camcorder is pointed at a white surface and the colour temperature determined and stored. This system isn't fooled by different colours in the scene.

This scene is lit by fluorescent lighting, which can fool the camcorder's white balance system. This shot is what the camcorder would record if a daylight (5,600K) setting were selected instead of the fluorescent setting.

When the fluorescent setting is selected, the green tinge is largely removed. If your camcorder has no pre-set for fluorescent lighting, you may be able to compensate by placing a magenta filter on the front of the lens (see Filters, p. 58).

LIGHTING PROBLEMS

 I recently recorded some brightly coloured fireworks, but on playback they aren't anywhere near as vibrant as I remember them.

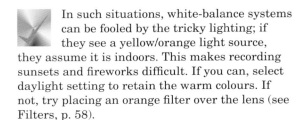 In such situations, white-balance systems can be fooled by the tricky lighting; if they see a yellow/orange light source, they assume it is indoors. This makes recording sunsets and fireworks difficult. If you can, select daylight setting to retain the warm colours. If not, try placing an orange filter over the lens (see Filters, p. 58).

The camcorder detects the warm colours in the fireworks and suspects tungsten lighting. It thus boosts the blues to reduce the red, and washes out the colours. The dark sky also causes the camcorder to boost the light level, further burning out the points of light.

If you can, select a daylight setting, to help to retain the warm colours. Some exposure programs such as twilight (see p. 36–7) may also help.

 I am often asked to record weddings, but in church I sometimes have a problem with mixed lighting. The couple and the vicar are lit by tungsten lights, but the rest of the congregation is lit with window light. Is there a solution?

 Not a wholly satisfactory one. The camcorder cannot set a different white-balance setting for different parts of the scene, and has to choose one value or the other. In normal indoor situations, you should increase one light source at the expense of the other – for instance, close the curtains in a living room and boost the number of tungsten bulbs, or turn off the lights and shoot by the window.

One solution to the problem is careful composition. If the couple are under very strong tungsten light, crop in close on them (above) and set the indoor white-balance setting. When you record the congregation, use the daylight setting. Avoid wide shots that include both light sources. You may be able to solve the problem better if you are allowed to use a video light in the church (such as an 800W or 1,000W lamp). These can be balanced for daylight by placing a blue 'dichroic' filter in front of them. Bounce the light from the lamp on to a white umbrella or reflector, then on to the couple.

THE LENS

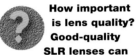 **How important is lens quality?** Good-quality SLR lenses can be expensive, especially fast zoom lenses. But my camcorder has an 8x zoom built in. Does this mean the lens quality is poor?

 There are two important differences between lens design for still cameras and for camcorders. First is the quality of the recording medium. Film has a much greater resolution than video, so lenses have to be superior to cope with the demands of the format. But the most important factor is the size of the image area the light has to be projected on to. SLR or 35mm cameras project on to a slide or negative that is 24mm x 36mm/1 x 1½ in – a surface area of 864mm²/1½ in². Camcorder imaging devices are much smaller, so camcorder lenses have to produce an image that is often 10 or 20 times smaller than the area of a 35mm slide or negative. It is a lot less costly to design and manufacture a lens that has to produce a good-quality image over a smaller area.

 How do focal lengths of camcorders relate to 35mm camera lenses?

Focal length (measured in millimetres) indicates the angle of view covered by a lens; the smaller the focal length, the wider the coverage. A camcorder's angle of view is determined by both focal length and the size of the CCD chip (see Recording an Image, p. 40). A very rough formula is: 3 x camcorder focal length/size of CCD in inches = 35mm SLR focal length. The table gives more accurate figures.

	Angle of view	¼in chip	⅓in chip	½in chip	⅔in chip	35mm equivalent
Typical wide-angle	46.0°	4.4mm	5.7mm	8.6mm	11mm	50mm
3x setting	15.3°	13.2mm	17.2mm	25.8mm	33mm	150mm
6x setting	7.6°	26.4mm	34.5mm	51.7mm	66mm	300mm
8x setting	5.7°	35.2mm	46.0mm	68.9mm	88mm	400mm
64x digital zoom	0.7°	281.6mm	368.0mm	551.7mm	710mm	3,200mm

E.g. A ⅓in chip camcorder with a 5.7–34.5mm focal range has the rough equivalent of a 50–300mm zoom on a still camera *(all figures approximate)*

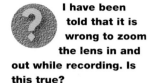

I have been told that it is wrong to zoom the lens in and out while recording. Is this true?

It isn't wrong to zoom the lens while recording, but it is a good idea to limit your use of the zoom. The main function of a zoom lens is to enable you to compose your subject perfectly. Zooming in and out can look messy – it's often much better to cut than to zoom from a wide-angle shot to a telephoto. Zoom shots do have their uses, however, particularly when showing a wide location. Start with a close-up detail, then slowly zoom out to reveal the setting. For these shots, it is best to use a tripod.

Slowly zooming out from a close-up (*left*) to reveal a scene (*below*) gives you the opportunity to identify the subject, then show the surroundings. It is often more effective than zooming in, as more of the scene is being revealed throughout the shot, and this helps retain the viewer's interest.

CLOSE-UP SHOTS

I want to focus on a very close subject, and have been told that the macro facility can help me do this. What is macro?

Camcorders are capable of focusing on very close subjects – much closer than most still camera lenses can. The majority can focus on subjects only a few millimetres away from the end of the lens. The term given to close focusing, where a tiny subject fills the frame, is 'macro'. Technically, 'macro' describes any image where the subject is the same size on the recording medium (either CCD, negative or slide) as it is in real life, but the term is often used to refer to any close-up recording.

Most camcorders offer macro at the wide-angle end of the zoom only. This means you have to get very close to the subject for it to fill the frame, and with subjects such as insects this can be tricky. Some camcorders offer auto-macro, but with others you have to select macro manually. Focus is then fixed and you have to move the camcorder to focus the image.

I want to use macro facility to video flowers in my garden, but I find it difficult to keep the subject sharp. Is there any way I can make it easier?

The closer the lens is focused, the smaller the area in front of and behind the subject that is sharp (see Depth of Field, p. 38), so correct focusing is critical if your picture is to be as sharp as the one below. Both your camcorder and the subject must remain still: if the wind is blowing, for example, you won't be able to record a sharp image. Place your camcorder on a tripod and ask someone to hold the flower in place. Alternatively, you could tape the stem of the flower to a firm structure out of shot. A black piece of card behind the flower makes for a much less cluttered background.

I have used macro facility to video spider's webs in my garden. However, I find the web is almost invisible on screen.

Subjects such as spiders' webs are delicate and don't show up too well against a dark background. The best thing to do is backlight the web by pointing a video light at it from below – making sure that the light doesn't shine directly into the camcorder's lens. If the light is tungsten-balanced, place a blue filter over it.

EXPOSURE

How much light does my camcorder need to record a reasonable image?

Most camcorders can record in candle-light, but may need several hundred lux to record a good-quality image. As a few hundred lux is quite low (see below), camcorders will cope well with most lighting conditions.

Bright snow scene	Up to 100,000 lux
Bright summer day	Around 40,000 lux
Clear winter day	Around 12,000 lux
Dull day	Around 4,000 lux
Overcast day	Around 3,000 lux
Room in daylight	Around 1,000 lux
Room at night	100 lux
Candlelight	less than 10 lux

Levels of light differ by hundreds of thousands of lux, a lux being a measure of light. Camcorders have been designed to record in levels as low as 10 lux, though the quality will not be perfect.

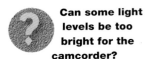

Can some light levels be too bright for the camcorder?

Lux levels of 75,000–100,000 can be too high. The picture may suffer from washed-out colours and overexposure. The best solution is to place a neutral-density (ND) filter on the lens. This simply absorbs some of the light.

When shooting in very bright conditions, a neutral density filter will prevent overexposure.

 My camcorder has manual iris, but I tend to use my camcorder on fully automatic. How useful is manual iris?

 As with the human eye, the iris is a circular opening that can increase or decrease in size depending on the intensity of the light hitting it. The most important use of manual iris is to regulate exposure, the amount of light entering the camera and falling on the CCD. In dark conditions, the iris opens to allow more light in; in bright light its size is reduced. If too much light hits the CCD, the image is overexposed, and the colours washed out; if too little light hits it, the image is dark and underexposed.

Autoexposure systems are designed to measure the amount of light in a scene, then set the correct iris. This is easy when there is a fairly even light intensity, but difficult when there is very high contrast between highlights and shadows. In these conditions, the camcorder may set the wrong exposure level. If you have a fully automatic system, there is little you can do about it, but with manual iris you can reduce or increase the size of the opening until you see in the viewfinder the correct exposure for your chosen subject.

MANUAL EXPOSURE

My camcorder has a backlight compensation button. What is it for?

In most situations, the camcorder's auto-exposure system measures the light and sets the appropriate iris. However, one situation frequently causes problems. When the subject is against a much brighter background, the camcorder tends to underexpose, causing the subject to silhouette. The solution is to use backlight compensation.

When the background is very bright, the camcorder might set an iris that doesn't let in enough light to expose the subject correctly. In extreme circumstances, this can cause it to silhouette.

If your camcorder has a backlight compensation (BLC) button, pressing this opens the iris. This exposes the subject better, but burns out the background.

Left: Sports mode freezes high-speed subjects for slow-motion.

Below left: Twilight mode prevents the atmosphere being lost when shooting in low light.

Below: Portrait mode blurs potentially distracting backgrounds.

 What are program modes?

 Program modes give limited control over exposure by allowing you to select an appropriate recording mode:

Sports – selects a fast shutter (see Fast Shutters, p. 42), producing blur-free freeze frames for slow-motion playback. With very fast shutters, subjects can appear to move jerkily.

Portrait – selects widest iris to blur background (see Depth of Field, p. 38). Use with telephoto lens for the best results.

Landscape – disregards light readings from top third of image to compensate for sky.

Twilight – doesn't increase exposure in low light. This helps retain atmosphere at dusk and enables recording of sunsets and fireworks.

Spotlight – in very high-contrast light situations measures exposure from the highlights, not the whole scene, to prevent highlights burning out.

DEPTH OF FIELD

What is depth of field?

When the camcorder focuses on a subject, some of the scene in front of and behind this point is also in focus. The distance from the furthest point in focus to the nearest is called the depth of field. Three factors affect depth of field: the size of the iris, the lens setting being used and the distance of the subject from the camcorder.

Your shots have the widest depth of field when you have a combination of wide-angle lens, distant subject and narrow iris. If you record a scene where you want everything to be in focus, it is best to shoot in bright conditions (as this will set a narrow iris) using the wide-angle end of the zoom.

Narrow depths of field enable you to isolate your subject from its surroundings – when much of the scene is blurred, the eye is naturally drawn to sharp subjects in the frame. For a narrow-focus shot, use a combination of telephoto lens, close subject and wide iris.

What are 'pull focus' and 'throw focus'?

In any scene you record, there may be a number of subjects you could focus on, but unlike still photography, where you have to focus then press the shutter release, in video you can change the point of focus while recording. This technique is often used to move the viewer's attention from one subject to another. Classic examples include shifting between two people having a conversation or argument and shifting focus to a new subject as it enters the frame.

Moving the point of focus closer to you is called pull focus. Refocusing on a more distant point is called throw focus. For both shots you need manual focus – an older-style focusing ring is best. Ideally, you should set the camcorder on a tripod for pull- and throw-focus shots.

Throw-focus shots are often used to introduce a scene. A telephoto lens is used to guarantee a narrow depth of field, and the lens is focused on a very near subject, so the background is completely blurred. The focusing ring is then twisted until the main subject is sharp.

RECORDING AN IMAGE

What is a CCD?

For the camcorder to record images on videotape, it first has to convert light entering the lens into an electrical signal. This is the job of the CCD (charge-coupled device). The CCD is a silicon chip made up of thousands of tiny picture elements (pixels). These are sensitive to light, and when light hits a pixel it sends out an electrical charge – the greater the light intensity, the greater the charge. Each pixel is covered by a tiny coloured filter – three different-coloured pixels working together to form one element of the picture. There are around 500 or 600 horizontal rows of pixels, depending on the TV standard being used (see Compatibility, p. 14). Each line is made up of as many pixels as can be crammed into the space.

FRAME 1

FRAME 2

If the CCD records still pictures, how does the camcorder record a moving image?

The CCD records a series of still images (50 per second for PAL and SECAM, 60 for NTSC). These are called 'fields'. For each field, only half of the pixels (each alternate line on the CCD) are supplied with a charge and register an image. For the next ⅟₅₀th sec, the other lines are supplied with a charge. A TV interlaces two consecutive fields to form a high quality 'frame'. The light from each frame remains on the retina for a fraction of a second, presenting an illusion of continuous movement.

My recordings have white spots on the right of the frame. This is more noticeable when shooting at night. Is my camcorder faulty?

 It is possible that one or a number of pixels on the CCD has failed. Each CCD carries hundreds of thousands of pixels, but the inevitable dud ones are normally masked by substituting the signal from a neighbouring good pixel. Sometimes pixels wear out, and if your camcorder is still under warranty take it back and get it repaired.

Is it possible for a camcorder's recording system to wear out? My camcorder's picture has severely deteriorated over the few years I've had it.

Before CCDs were incorporated into camcorders, light rays were converted to electrical signals using pick-up tubes. Unlike CCDs, these are not so resilient to shocks or to being pointed at bright lights. If yours is a tube camcorder, the tubes may need replacing. If it is a CCD camcorder, try cleaning the video heads. If this doesn't work, take the camcorder to be serviced – the CCD will not have worn, unless it is faulty, but it's possible that other parts have worn.

FRAME 3

FRAME 4

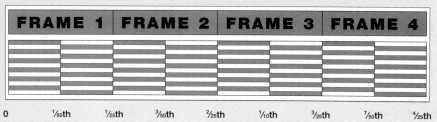

FRAME 1	FRAME 2	FRAME 3	FRAME 4

0    $\frac{1}{50}$th $\frac{1}{25}$th $\frac{3}{50}$th $\frac{2}{25}$th $\frac{1}{10}$th $\frac{3}{25}$th $\frac{7}{50}$th $\frac{4}{25}$th

Only half of the CCD (each alternate line) registers an image at any one time. Two consecutive images (fields) are interlaced to form a complete frame.

FAST SHUTTERS

What are fast shutters for?

In still photography, fast shutters are used to 'freeze' fast action: when the shutter is open only briefly, fast subjects don't move very far, so there is no blur. When you press the fast shutter button on a camcorder, a lot of action is unrecorded between each field (see box below), and moving subjects appear to move jerkily – so fast shutters are appropriate when you want to play back action in slow motion or study your video without the subject being blurred. They are less appropriate when playing back at normal speed. Some camcorders can set shutters as fast as $\frac{1}{10,000}$ sec.

How do fast shutters work?

Camcorders don't have actual shutters – shutter speed refers to the amount of time an electrical charge is supplied to the CCD during the recording of each field (see Recording an Image p. 40). The CCD needs a charge to record an image.

As there are 50 (or 60 for NTSC) fields per second, the standard camcorder shutter speed is $\frac{1}{50}$ sec. At this speed, the CCD records continuously. When you select a fast shutter – e.g. $\frac{1}{500}$ sec – each field is recorded for $\frac{1}{500}$ sec only. The rest of the time, the CCD records nothing. Each field is then copied on to the tape 10 times to make up the $\frac{1}{50}$ sec, so there is no blank tape.

Above left: With a standard shutter speed, freeze-frame images of fast action will blur.

When you use a high-speed shutter, far less light has the chance to enter the camcorder and reach the CCD. In low light conditions, in order to achieve correct exposure, the camcorder has to increase the current (and sensitivity to light) to the pixels. This is known as 'boosting the gain'. The resulting image generally looks grainy (*above left*). In bright light, the camcorder doesn't have to boost the gain, and the quality is fine (*above right*).

FRAME 1	FRAME 2	FRAME 3

| 0 | ¹⁄₅₀₀th | ¹⁄₅₀th | ¹⁄₂₅th | ³⁄₅₀th | ²⁄₂₅th | ¹⁄₁₀th | ³⁄₂₅th |

TRANSFERRING TO TAPE

How are images from the CCD transferred to videotape?

Each of the hundreds of thousands of pixels on the CCD corresponds to the colour and intensity of the light at that particular section of the image. These individual charges emerge from the CCD 50 or 60 times a second as a continuous stream of electrical pulses (see Recording an Image, p. 40). This is the video signal. It is processed by the camcorder's electronic circuitry and sent to the cylindrical video head drum.

This video head drum spins 2,250 times per second. It contains tiny video 'heads' that are capable of writing information on to the tape. The tape is wrapped around the head drum, and the heads record an image by writing the video signal on to the tape, which is done by magnetizing the metal coating of the tape. The sound meanwhile is picked up by the microphone and amplified before being sent to the head drum's audio heads. It is then laid on to the tape at the same time as the video signal.

Cylindrical head drum from a Hi8 camcorder. The tape is wrapped around the drum, and the heads record an image by magnetizing the metal coating of the tape. A and B denote the two video heads.

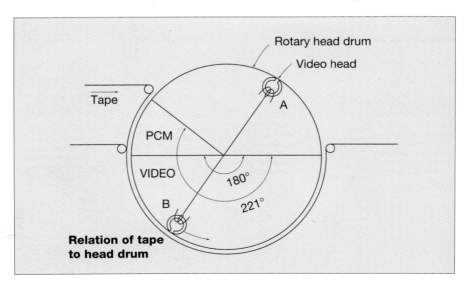

How are sound and pictures stored on videotape?

Different sound systems store the video and audio signals in different places on the tape. All video signals are laid in the centre of the tape by the spinning head drum. VHS hi-fi and 8mm sound are recorded in the same place on the tape as the video, but at a deeper level. VHS linear mono is recorded not by the camcorder's spinning head drum but by a fixed head that runs along the edge of the tape.

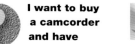

I want to buy a camcorder and have noticed that many have both long play (LP) and standard play (SP). Is there a considerable drop in quality in LP mode?

Most camcorders feature long play (LP) as well as standard play (SP) modes. In long play, the tape speed is halved, which allows you to record twice as much information on a cassette. However, as twice the information has to be laid on the same amount of tape as in standard play, there is inevitably some quality loss. Picture quality is only slightly affected, and this is crucial only if you intend to edit your videos.

As quality is lost every time you copy, aim to start off with the best-quality original. If you are using a VHS mono camcorder, which has only a linear mono track, the quality of this is noticeably reduced in LP mode, so stick to SP.

This diagram shows where sound and picture information is stored on 8mm and VHS tape.

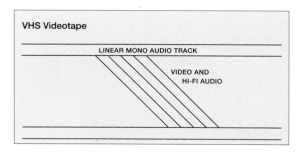

VHS Videotape

LINEAR MONO AUDIO TRACK

VIDEO AND HI-FI AUDIO

8 mm Videotape

VIDEO AND FM STEREO

PCM STEREO

BACKSPACING

My camcorder doesn't always end shots at the point I pressed the pause button. When I play my recording back, I find that the end of what someone was saying is cut off. Is the camcorder faulty?

When you press the camcorder's record button, three things are recorded on the tape – video, sound and something called a control track. The control track consists of a series of pulses laid down on the tape at regular intervals – imagine an electronic version of the sprocket holes on the side of a roll of film. The camcorder locks on to this control track during playback, enabling it to keep the playback heads correctly aligned. If two pulses were irregularly spaced, the camcorder would struggle for a moment, resulting in interference on the screen.

When you press the pause button, the camcorder backspaces, which rolls back the tape a second or two.

When you press the record button, the camcorder pre-rolls the tape a few frames to lock on to the previous track's control pulses.

It then starts recording. The result is a missing few frames from the end of the first shot and the same from the start of the second.

To ensure a clean start to your video, record a few seconds in a quiet location with the lens cap on. This provides a control track for the first shot to lock on to.

Pre-roll

To prevent control pulses recording at irregular intervals every time you press the pause button, the camcorder incorporates backspace facility. When you pause the camcorder, the tape rolls back slightly (the actual time varies between camcorders, but it's generally a second or two). When you start recording the second shot, the camcorder rolls the tape forward for a few frames without recording. This is the pre-roll – it does this to lock on to the previous shot's control track. It then starts recording – but at a point before you paused the previous shot. The result is a few missing frames from the end of the first shot and the start of the second. To compensate for this, add a little time on to the start and end of each shot.

Press record/pause here

Rollback

Recording starts here

EXTRA FACILITIES

How does an interval timer work?

Interval timers are found on only a few camcorder models. When in this mode, the camcorder records a short burst of video – normally a couple of seconds or so – at regular intervals. The length of this interval varies from model to model, but typically a camcorder might record a short burst of a scene once every 30 seconds or once every minute.

One of the most useful applications of this feature is time lapse: set the camcorder on a tripod and let it record over several hours. You can then record a flower opening in the space of a few seconds, or the sun travelling rapidly across the sky. An interval timer can also be used for basic animation. Between each burst of recording, you move your subject – a model or a child's toy – so that it appears to move across the frame. The result will be very jerky, however.

My camcorder has video insert facility. What is this exactly?

Video insert facility allows you to record over a recording without causing interference at the end of the shot (see Insert Editing, p. 104). It does this by recording new video without recording a control track (see Backspacing, p. 46). Instead, it uses the existing control track, so there must already be a control track on the tape – which will be the control track of the video you are recording over.

How useful is a self-timer?

When you activate the self-timer, the camcorder waits a few seconds before it starts to record. This enables you to appear in the shot yourself. Some models let you set the length of time for which the camcorder records before it pauses. The feature is of very limited creative use, as you can't monitor the image to see if people move out of the frame.

Why do camcorders have remote controls? I have noticed that most 8mm camcorders feature remote control, but most VHS-Cs don't. Are they important?

Remote controls are used mainly to operate the camcorder during playback. They are not essential, but they are convenient, particularly if your camcorder has tiny control buttons.

The reason 8mm camcorders are more likely to have remote controls is that VHS-C tapes can be played directly in a VHS video recorder using an adaptor. You can then use the VCR's remote control to control playback. However, 8mm camcorders cannot be played back on a VHS VCR, hence the need for a remote control.

The big advantage of insert edit comes with VHS family camcorders (see p. 12), which have mono soundtracks recorded separately from the picture. This means you can insert new video without recording over the continuous sound.

IN-CAMERA TITLING

How do titling systems for camcorders work?

There are two kinds of titling facility: character generators and digital frame stores. Character generators enable you to type a simple caption using either an add-on keypad or various buttons on your camcorder. Character generators are very limited in the styles and type sizes they can use, but the quality is more consistent than with digital frame stores. With digital frame store, when you press the frame store button, the camcorder takes a snapshot of the scene. Either the dark or light parts of the image (you choose) are captured by the frame store, while the rest of the image is transparent. If you point the camcorder at a black title on white, the black title can be stored, and superimposed over another image.

The easiest way of adding a title is to use a camcorder with a built-in titling system.

My camcorder does not have any titling facilities. Is it possible to include normal titles without buying an add-on titling unit?

The easiest way of adding a title is simply to create one by writing or using transfer lettering on a contrasting cardboard background. You won't be able to superimpose captions over live recordings, but you can rub transfer lettering on to clear acetate sheets and place these over still photographs at the beginning of your recording (see Video Stills, p. 130).

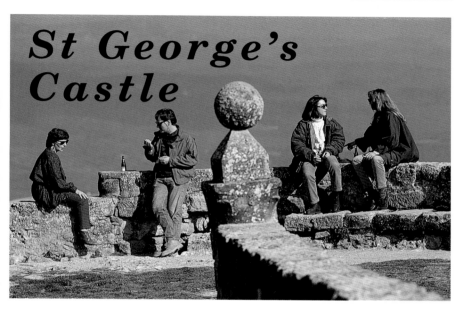

St George's Castle

 Some of my titles look better than others. Are there any useful guidelines when it comes to creating titles?

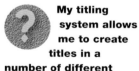 It is important to choose lettering that is easy to read and large enough not to break up on screen. Capital letters have more impact, but they are more difficult to read than lower case letters. Don't choose a fancy typeface or thin italics – a solid, bold style looks best. Find a portion of the scene that is not cluttered (above) or, better still, a single colour.

My titling system allows me to create titles in a number of different colours. Are some colours better than others?

Choose a colour that contrasts sharply with the background colour. If you are superimposing over sky, choose either a dark colour, such as red or black, or, if the sky is a deep blue, you may be able to get away with white. White on a dark background stands out the most, but you have to make sure the background is very dark, otherwise the lettering will be lost. If you are creating titles after you have recorded the image, or are shooting titles over still pictures or arranged backgrounds, use the TV as a monitor, rather than the camcorder's viewfinder.

VIEWFINDERS

I understand that some camcorders have colour viewfinders, while others have black and white. What are the advantages of each?

Most camcorder viewfinders consist of a tiny black and white (mono) TV. Just like conventional TVs, they use reasonably good-quality picture tubes. Colour picture tubes would be a lot more expensive and more of a drain on the battery power, so colour monitors in camcorders use liquid crystal display (LCD) technology. There is a limit to the number of pixels (see Recording an Image, p. 40) that can be crammed on to an LCD, making the overall quality much lower than on mono viewfinders.

To solve this problem, some camcorder manufacturers have built in a large colour monitor, some as large as 10cm/4 in square (see below). Colour monitors are particularly good for checking colour balance and for observing the effects of coloured filters. Because of the quality, mono viewfinders are good for manual focusing.

A number of camcorders now have large colour LCD monitors built in.

Although camcorder viewfinders are fixed, detachable eyepieces are common.

 There is a line like a hair in my viewfinder, but it doesn't appear on recordings. What can I do about it?

 It may actually be a hair inside the viewfinder. On many camcorders you can take the end of the viewfinder off – simply twist the viewfinder just below the eyepiece, then pull. It may be that the hair is easy to get at and you can remove it. If it is in an inaccessible part of the viewfinder, however, you will have to take it to a service engineer. The alternative is to do nothing; it may be irritating, but it isn't doing any harm.

 When I power up my camcorder, I get flashing symbols in my viewfinder. What is going on?

 Some camcorders have automatic fault diagnosis circuitry built in. When the camcorder develops a fault, the various combinations of flashing symbols tell the service engineer what is wrong, and this makes finding the fault a lot quicker and easier. Take the camcorder to a qualified service engineer to have it checked out.

 What is a sportsfinder?

 Although the type of viewfinder is fixed with camcorders, some manufacturers supply interchangeable eyepieces. A sportsfinder contains a magnification lens that simply increases the size of the image on the viewfinder. The advantage of this is that you don't need to press your eye against the eyepiece to see the image – you can see well enough from a few inches away.

ACCESSORIES AND SOUND

TRIPODS AND SUPPORTS

 I bought a palmcorder because I wanted to video plays and live bands, which means I'm recording for a long time. Despite its being so light, my arm still gets tired. Should I get a tripod?

 If you record plays or live music, a tripod is a must whatever your camcorder. The tripod needs to be sturdy, but just as important is the tripod head – the moving section between the legs and the camcorder. The best reasonably priced heads are fluid-effect heads.

A tripod is the best way to be sure of obtaining a steady image. Look for one with a smooth-moving fluid-effect head.

 I have a tripod for when I am recording near my home or anywhere I can get to in a car, but it is too cumbersome to carry far. Are there any alternatives?

 A number of camcorder supports are available. A chestpod, for instance, is a harness that fits around the shoulders and waist – it gives excellent support, but is conspicuous. A pistol grip screws into the camcorder's tripod thread and gives added stability; but probably the best portable support for a camcorder is the monopod, a solid pole that screws into the camcorder's base. Good monopods telescope into themselves, like a car aerial.

I understand that both tripod dollies and the Steadicam JR are used for steady, moving shots. But which is better?

A tripod dolly consists of a frame with three wheels that fits on to the bottom of your tripod. It enables you to move the tripod on smooth surfaces so you can record moving shots without jerkiness.

The Steadicam JR is a cleverly designed grip that screws into the camcorder's tripod thread. It has no contact with the floor and relies on the distribution of weights and counter weights to keep the camcorder level. It also contains a mono LCD monitor so you can walk about without having to place your eye to the viewfinder.

Dollies are useful when the ground is smooth and you know exactly where you want to move the camcorder to and from. If the ground is not smooth, you have to lay down planks of wood to run the dolly along. The Steadicam is more convenient when the ground is bumpy or when you are following moving subjects and do not know their movements in advance.

A tripod dolly (*below left*) will help to ensure a steady image if you are recording on the move, but it has its limitations. The Steadicam JR (*below right*) offers greater mobility in the same situation.

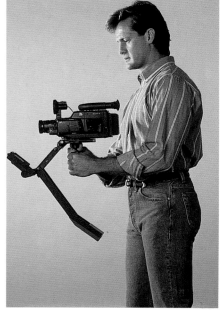

FILTERS

 **I have a large number of filters for my SLR camera, but they are all too large to fit my camcorder. Is it possible to adapt them, or do I have to buy a new set?**

 As long as your camcorder has a filter thread, you should have no difficulty attaching your SLR filters to your camcorder lens. You need to get hold of a special adaptor ring from a photographic outlet. This has two differently sized threads placed back to back. Your filters screw into the larger ring, and the smaller ring attaches to the end of your camcorder lens.

A UV filter reduces haze and protects your lens.

 I have been advised to buy a skylight or UV (ultraviolet) filter for my camcorder. What are these exactly, and which is better?

 A filter is a piece of glass or plastic placed in front of the lens to modify the light passing through it. Among the most basic are skylight and UV (ultraviolet) filters. Both cut down the blue cast on distant subjects that can be caused by haze. Their primary function is to protect the front element of your lens. It is a good idea to keep one permanently attached.

What effect does a polarizing filter have?

 There are three important effects: reducing reflection on shiny surfaces, such as glass and water (but not metal); deepening blue skies; and, like a skylight filter, cutting down on haze. The effect of the filter is increased or reduced according to how it is positioned. If your camcorder has inner focusing, the act of focusing will rotate any filter placed on the lens. With a polarizer, this means you have to focus before correctly positioning the filter.

How do colour filters affect the camcorder's white-balance system?

Some camcorders measure white balance through the lens, while others use an external white sensor. If the camcorder uses an external sensor, placing a filter over the end of the lens has no effect on the white balance. If white balance is measured through the lens, the camcorder attempts to compensate for the filter by boosting the opposite colour, reducing the filter's effect. Camcorders may not fully compensate for strong colour filters.

I have seen dramatic moonlit shots on TV. Do I need special equipment to record similar shots?

What you are probably seeing is a movie trick known as 'day for night'. The shot is actually recorded during the day, but a blue filter is placed over the lens. The shot works best if the sun is in the frame – with the blue filter, the sun resembles a full moon. Underexposing slightly enhances the effect.

Place a blue filter on the lens and narrow the iris to create a day-for-night effect (*below*).

LENS CONVERTERS

Above: Teleconverters enable you to fill the frame with a small, distant subject.

Right: Teleconverters screw into the camcorder's filter thread.

What is a lens converter?

A lens converter is an additional lens that screws on to the end of your normal camcorder lens, modifying its focal length by a set amount. This amount is known as the add-on lens's conversion factor. If a converter with a conversion factor of 2x were attached to the lens of a camcorder with a typical 11–88mm focal range (see The Lens, p. 30), the telephoto focal length of the camcorder would double to 176mm. Converters that increase the focal length are known as teleconverters. Converters that reduce the focal length are called wide-angle converters.

Why does the picture go dark at the edges when I use a teleconverter?

 This effect is known as vignetting, and is most pronounced when you are not using the lens at its extreme telephoto setting. If the screen always goes dark at the edge of the frame, the teleconverter is poorly made.

 I have been told that my autofocus system won't work if I use a tele-converter. Is this true?

 On camcorders with active autofocus systems, the AF will not work with a converter. Switch the camcorder to manual focus and set it to infinity. Focus the image using the converter's manual focus ring. If the viewfinder image is dark, you will see better with an add-on monitor.

 I have seen camcorders boasting 64x zooms. Is this better than buying a long teleconverter?

 Camcorders achieve extreme telephoto settings, such as 64x, by electronically enlarging the central portion of the image. The greater the enlargement, the lower the number of pixels that make up the image, so at 64x the image quality is very poor. There is less reduction in quality with a teleconverter.

 I recently saw an interesting effect in an old movie – the frame became circular and the subject became completely distorted.

 This is achieved with a fish-eye converter. This is attached to the wide-angle end of the lens and results in a very short focal length and an extremely wide field of view (as much as 180°). Subjects at the edge of the frame appear very distorted, and subjects that are very close are distorted most.

A fish-eye lens is often used to show or exaggerate a person's point of view, suggesting that they are hallucinating, drunk or disorientated.

ADD-ON LIGHTS

Do I need to use an add-on light only in very dark conditions, or is it useful at other times?

Although camcorders can record in extremely low light, picture quality suffers at low levels. Add-on (video) lights ensure the subject is evenly lit. Lights can also be used on dull days to pick out your main subject from its background. This is particularly useful when your subject is very close to the camcorder and the background is cluttered, and when you are shooting a backlit subject. A video light gets round the need to use backlight compensation, as it brightens up the foreground subject so that it is no longer darker than the background. Video lights are like indoor light, so use a blue filter in front of a video light when using it outdoors.

Lights can be used for good effect in fairly bright conditions too. They can brighten up an outdoor subject when it is heavily backlit – or a subject that is in shadow.

My camcorder doesn't have an accessory shoe. Can I still use an add-on light?

At one time virtually all camcorders had an accessory shoe on their top-plate to which a light or microphone could be attached. But with the drive towards ever-smaller camcorders, the accessory shoe was one of the first things to go. If your camcorder is without a shoe, it should still have a tripod thread on its underside. Accessory brackets can be screwed into this thread and feature one or more accessory shoes. If you buy one of these, you can then use a video light.

I want to buy an add-on light, but am worried about the battery power. I get little enough recording time as it is.

You can soften the effect of direct lighting by placing a diffuser over your light. Heatproof diffusion material can be bought from professional photography shops.

Camcorder lights use a lot of battery power, but the better models run off their own rechargeable battery rather than draining the camcorder's. If you use a light often, choose one with its own power source. If you frequently pause the camcorder, then start to record again, switch the light off as soon as you pause rather than leaving it switched on. Better lamps can also be powered from the mains.

When using my add-on light, I sometimes find that areas of the scene – in particular people's faces – can be too bright. Is there any way of preventing this?

The closer the subject to the camcorder, the stronger it will be illuminated by the video light. As most lights give out a constant amount of light, close subjects can be very brightly lit. If the background is very bright too, the camcorder's exposure system will simply narrow the iris to expose the scene correctly. If the background is quite dark, however, the exposure system might set a slightly wider iris to compensate. This can lead to areas of the main subject being overbright, resulting in the burn-out – or 'hotspots' – you describe. Hotspots are only really a problem with highly reflective subjects, which unfortunately include skin. Either stand further back from your subject and crop in close by zooming in to a slightly narrower lens setting, or diffuse the light in some way to make it less harsh. You can buy dedicated diffusers for some models.

VIDEOTAPE

How do blank VHS and S-VHS tapes differ? Is it possible to record on S-VHS tape in a VHS camcorder or vice versa?

S-VHS tapes use a better formulation to pack in more magnetic particles, to better hold the greater amount of information inherent in the hi-band format. You can record on to S-VHS tape in a VHS VCR with very good results – but you won't get S-VHS quality. It would probably be better to save money and buy a pro grade VHS tape. If you place a VHS tape in an S-VHS VCR or camcorder, the machine will spot this and only record a VHS signal. It detects whether it is S-VHS or VHS because S-VHS has an extra hole in its shell. If you make a hole in the same place on a good-quality VHS tape, it will record an S-VHS signal. Manufacturers don't recommend this, as they claim VHS tape doesn't have the capacity to record an S-VHS signal.

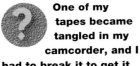

One of my tapes became tangled in my camcorder, and I had to break it to get it out. Can I repair it?

You can buy dedicated tape splicers from electrical shops, or you can find a facilities house that repairs tapes for you. Because the continuous control track will be broken at this point, you are likely to get interference at the break point.

I remember two-hour audiotapes being more delicate than C90s. Is the same true of long-running videotapes?

E240s (four-hour VHS) use a thinner base than E180s, so are naturally more delicate. However, your VCR should be able to cope with four-hour tapes without damaging them. Three-hour tapes often work out to be better value in terms of cost per minute's recording time.

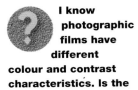

I know photographic films have different colour and contrast characteristics. Is the same true of videotape?

Tape quality is important, but it doesn't have the same characteristics as film. The colour is determined by the colour balance circuitry and the electronic chroma (colour) part of the picture signal. Poor-quality tapes can generate electronic 'picture noise', which can create a 'grainier', less sharp image.

If possible, store your tapes in heavy protective cases.

What is the best way of storing videotapes?

Stack cassettes upright in their boxes and insert them flap first into the box to protect the tape. Keep them away from dust, smoke and moisture in an environment that has a fairly constant temperature. Do not place them next to mains-operated equipment or magnetic sources such as loudspeakers, as this can wipe the information. If you send them through the post, use plastic bubblewrap, and avoid using any shredded fibres, as these can pollute the tape.

There are so many names for grades of tape – super high grade, pro grade and so on – which is the best?

There are no official standards for different videotape grades, so manufacturers can call them what they like. Most reputable companies stick to a system such as: standard, high grade, extra high grade and pro. If you have the funds, it's better to opt for the more expensive tapes – they tend to wear better and are the most strongly constructed. As a general rule, choose brand names that you know from audio tape, camcorders and VCRs.

SHOOTING ACCESSORIES

Camcorders don't have interchangeable viewfinders, but add-on colour monitors are available.

My camcorder has a mono viewfinder, and I would like to upgrade to colour. Is this possible, or would I need to buy a new camcorder?

No camcorder manufacturer has yet introduced interchangeable viewfinders for its camcorders – so if your camcorder has a mono viewfinder you can't swap it for a colour version. However, unless you are worried about the extra bulk, you can solve your problem by buying an add-on LCD (liquid crystal display) monitor. Some of these monitors are also TV sets, so you get twice the benefit.

LCD monitors come in various sizes – typically 5cm/2 in, 7.5cm/3 in and 10cm/4 in screens. Two screen types are used: active matrix and passive matrix. Passive matrix are cheaper, but give poorer-quality images. Active matrix, typically those sold by the camcorder manufacturers, often cost three times as much as passive versions. If your camcorder has an accessory shoe, you can mount the monitor on this. Monitors are particularly useful if you are using your camcorder on a tripod.

Marine housings enable you to take your camcorder underwater – but use one only if you are already competent underwater.

 I would like to video marine life. Do I need a special waterproof camcorder, or can my own camcorder be modified?

Waterproof camcorders are available, but you can obtain underwater camcorder housings for most models. Hard cases are more expensive than lightweight models, but they enable you to go down to a much greater depth. Consider taking your camcorder in the sea only if you are suitably competent underwater.

I have read of an attachment that enables the camcorder to video around corners. How does this work?

The candid-angle lens attachment enables you to see around corners, so you can video your subject without their knowing.

A candid-angle lens attachment enables you to video at 90° to the direction you are facing. It screws on to the lens just like a normal teleconverter – in fact, the candid-angle lens is designed to look like a teleconverter, so it doesn't draw attention to itself. Inside the attachment is a mirror angled at 45° to the front element of the lens. A circular opening in its side allows light from your right or left to hit the mirror and be reflected into the camcorder's lens.

RECORDING SOUND

How does a camcorder record sound?

Sound picked up by the camcorder's microphone is stored on the tape along with the video and the control track. Most camcorders feature an automatic gain control (AGC), which reduces the recording level in noisy conditions and amplifies the sound in quiet locations. Unfortunately, in most camcorders, this feature cannot be overridden.

Are some camcorders better at recording sound than others?

All camcorder microphones work by turning vibrations in the form of sound waves into a signal that can be stored magnetically on the tape and transformed back into sound waves later. But the sound-recording systems differ between different models.

Camcorders in the VHS family use two recording systems – all record linear mono, but only camcorders marked 'stereo' have stereo soundtracks. 8mm camcorders feature either FM mono or FM stereo tracks. In addition, some Hi8 camcorders have stereo tracks known as PCM. These give high-quality digital sound. The table below clarifies the various differences.

SYSTEM	FOUND ON	WHERE ON TAPE	ADVANTAGES	DISADVANTAGES
Linear mono	All VHS family	Edge of tape	Can be re-recorded separately	Poor quality
FM mono	Cheaper 8mm	With video signal	Better quality than linear mono	Can't be re-recorded independently of video
8mm FM stereo	Better 8mm and Hi8 models	With video signal	Separation between left and right tracks; good quality	More expensive than mono systems; can't be re-recorded independently of video
VHS hi-fi stereo	Better VHS family	With video signal	Can retain location sound on hi-fi tracks, and re-record on linear mono track	More expensive than mono systems
PCM stereo	Some Hi8 models	Independently of picture	Very high quality; can be re-recorded independently	Expensive

What is frequency response?

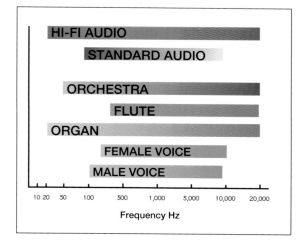

Sound travels through the air in wave-shaped patterns. The closer these waves are together, the deeper the sound. The number of waves a sound creates per second is known as its frequency – if it creates 100 per second, it has a frequency of 100Hz. The better the recording system, the more faithfully it can reproduce a wide range of frequencies. The diagram below shows the frequency ranges of various sound sources.

Male voice: 100–8,000Hz
Female voice: 150–10,000Hz
Organ: 20–20,000Hz
Flute: 275–20,000Hz
Orchestra: 40–20,000Hz

Standard audio: 80–10,000Hz
Hi-fi audio 20–20,000Hz

HI-FI AUDIO

STANDARD AUDIO

ORCHESTRA

FLUTE

ORGAN

FEMALE VOICE

MALE VOICE

10 20   50   100   500   1,000   5,000   10,000   20,000

Frequency Hz

Can I add sound to my tapes without recording over the pictures?

Some camcorders feature a facility called audio dub. This allows you to re-record the soundtrack without also recording over the original picture. The table on p. 68 tells you where each soundtrack is recorded on the videotape, depending on the system you are using. If sound is recorded at the same time as the picture, it cannot be re-recorded independently without audio-dub.

The linear mono and PCM tracks can be audio dubbed. If a VHS camcorder has linear mono only, the entire soundtrack is replaced when you audio dub. But if it is hi-fi stereo, new sound is recorded on the mono track, and the original is retained on the stereo tracks.

SOUND ACCESSORIES

 In quiet locations, my camcorder picks up the sound of its own zoom and AF motors. Is there any way of preventing this?

Use an accessory microphone to eliminate handling noise. A windshield cuts down wind noise.

 This is more noticeable in quiet locations because the camcorder's audio AGC (see Recording Sound, p. 68) is turned right up, making it more sensitive to all sounds. The best solution is to use an accessory microphone. As this is isolated from the camcorder operations, it will not pick up unwanted handling noises.

 I have a lot of problems with wind noise when recording outside. What can I do about this?

 Whether using your camcorder's built-in microphone or an external microphone, you should fit a windshield whenever you are recording in windy locations. Windshields reduce the velocity of the wind falling on the microphone, cutting the rumble that wind causes.

Some camcorders have a noise-reduction switch. This reduces the low-frequency response, thus reducing wind noise, but it affects how faithfully low frequencies are recorded.

 My camcorder has no headphone socket. Does this mean I cannot monitor the sound being recorded?

 Although your camcorder has no headphone socket, it will have an audio out connection (even if it is part of a plug that contains audio and video). A good electrical store should be able to sell you a headphone adaptor to plug into your audio out. Make sure your headphones cover the ears completely, so you hear only what the camcorder is recording.

I like to record outdoor music. The problem is, the microphone picks up chatter from all around, not just the music. If I move closer, I cannot fit the band in. What should I do?

You need an add-on microphone that is highly sensitive to sounds coming from the front. The most important thing about microphones is their directional characteristics. Omnidirectional microphones are sensitive to sounds from all around, whereas cardioid and shotgun are biased towards noises from the front. You might get clearer sound by placing the microphone on a stand that is closer to the band than the camcorder.

I want to buy a clip-on microphone. Which is best, a wired or a radio microphone?

Each type has its own advantages and disadvantages. By attaching the microphone to your subject's tie or lapel, you will guarantee they can be heard properly. Wired microphones are considerably cheaper than radio microphones, and the sound quality tends to be more consistent. However, because there is a wire running between you and the subject, this makes them unsuitable for crowded locations. Radio microphones require a clean line of sight between the transmitter and the receiver.

RECORDING IN STEREO

What are the advantages of using stereo microphones rather than mono?

If you play back videos through a stereo TV with a good sound system, sound recorded in stereo has greater impact than sound recorded in mono. Stereo microphones contain two pick-ups set at 90° to each other. When recorded with a good-quality stereo microphone, sounds coming from the right are stronger in the right speaker, while sounds from the left are stronger in the left. But there is always some cross-over, with loud sounds on the right coming from the left speaker too, and vice versa.

Stereo microphones are useful for recording conversations. People on the left of the frame are louder out of the left speaker.

What is a mixer microphone?

A mixer microphone is an add-on stereo microphone that features an input for another sound source. The second sound source is usually either a narration microphone or a personal stereo. If it is a narration microphone, the normal stereo microphone records the sound in the location while you talk into the narration microphone. If it is a personal stereo, it enables you to add background music while recording. You have to record in a single take, however; if you pause the camcorder, the sound will jump. Mixer microphones may let you set relative volumes between the two sound sources so you can fade down the music if you want.

Using two microphones ensures that when a subject, such as a train, moves across the screen, the sound moves too, from speaker to speaker.

I have a stereo camcorder, but only one microphone input. I would like to be able to plug two separate mono microphones into my camcorder, to achieve a wide stereo separation. Is this possible?

Rather than use a single stereo microphone, you can record with two mono microphones either placed close together and at 90° to each other, or placed slightly apart. The two mono microphones need to be identical for the best effect. Placing the microphones slightly apart gives greater stereo separation than you get with one microphone. Even if you have a stereo camcorder, you will usually have only one microphone input. To solve this problem, buy a stereo microphone jack, which has inputs for two microphones and one output that plugs into your camcorder. You can use two mono microphones to record a conversation between two people, although the ping-pong effect between the two speakers can sound odd.

EDITING YOUR VIDEOS

PLAYING YOUR TAPES

My cousin has a VHS-C camcorder, and she plays her tapes through her TV by placing the cassettes in a VHS-sized cassette adaptor. Is it possible to buy an adaptor for my 8mm cassettes?

No. VHS-C cassettes use the same tape as VHS. The cassettes can be easily fitted into an adaptor for direct playback in a VHS VCR. But 8mm cassettes use a different width of tape and are incompatible with VHS.

VHS-C cassettes can be played directly in VHS VCRs using an adaptor; 8mm tapes cannot.

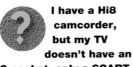

I have a Hi8 camcorder, but my TV doesn't have an S-socket, only a SCART socket. The TV manual says the SCART is not equipped for S-connection. So do I lose the quality advantage of the hi-band format?

You can connect your camcorder to your TV's SCART socket using the audio/video (A/V) outputs on your camcorder, but you will lose some of the hi-band quality. If your TV has no S-input, you can keep top quality by connecting the S-lead from the camcorder to an S-to-RGB converter. The output from this then connects to your VCR's SCART socket.

Running the S-lead through an S-to-RGB converter to a TV's SCART socket is the best way of retaining quality when using a TV without S-inputs. RGB splits the picture information into separate red, green and blue signals.

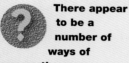 **There appear to be a number of ways of connecting my camcorder to my TV for playback. What are the differences?**

 All camcorders have standard A/V outputs, although the type of plug used (phono, 8-pin, 20-pin) varies between manufacturers. Hi-band camcorders also have an S-output that carries the high-quality hi-band signal. Many TVs now have S-input, and most have A/V inputs. If yours has neither, you can run the signal from the A/V outputs to an A/V-to-RF adaptor, and then to the TV's RF (aerial) socket. The quality is reduced, however, and stereo sound is rendered mono.

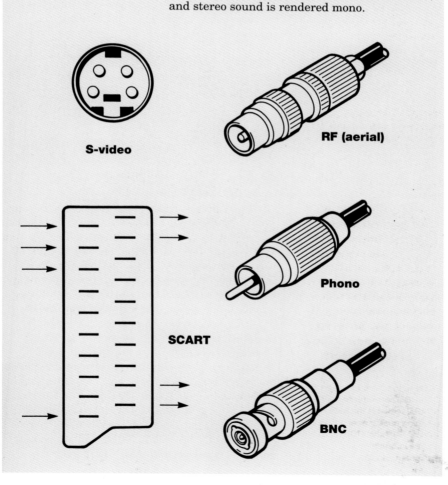

S-video

RF (aerial)

Phono

SCART

BNC

COPYING YOUR TAPES

What is the purpose of copying what I have recorded from my camcorder tape to a tape in my video recorder?

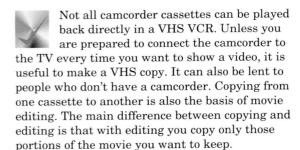

Not all camcorder cassettes can be played back directly in a VHS VCR. Unless you are prepared to connect the camcorder to the TV every time you want to show a video, it is useful to make a VHS copy. It can also be lent to people who don't have a camcorder. Copying from one cassette to another is also the basis of movie editing. The main difference between copying and editing is that with editing you copy only those portions of the movie you want to keep.

I want to copy the shots from my day out at the zoo. How do I connect my camcorder to my video recorder for copying, and what do I do once the two units are connected?

Connecting a camcorder to a VCR is similar to connecting it to a TV. The only difference is that unless you are using a hi-band VCR, it will not have an S-input. Even if your camcorder is hi-band, you will have to connect it to a VHS VCR using the standard A/V sockets (see Playing your Tapes, p. 76). Copying from your camcorder is similar to recording TV programmes off-air. Set the VCR tape to record/pause at the right point, and play/pause the camcorder where you want to begin recording. Release both pause buttons to copy. If your VCR has A/V inputs, the signal will be directed to channel '0'. If your camcorder has no A/V inputs, connect the signal to your VCR's RF (aerial) socket. Select a blank channel and tune it to the camcorder's frequency.

I have an S-VHS camcorder and a VHS video recorder. The VCR has a SCART socket that is not S-equipped; can I retain the playback quality by using an S-to-RGB camcorder?

Unfortunately not. Although TVs can handle RGB signals (see Playing your Tapes, p. 76), VCRs cannot. S-VHS carries more picture information than VHS. Although a large TV monitor can resolve this information, VHS tape should not be able to. Nevertheless, even through A/V connectors, a VHS copy of a hi-band recording is better quality than a VHS copy of a lo-band recording. An S-VHS copy of an S-VHS original is better still.

My friend has a recording of his child's party. It would be handy to copy this directly from his camcorder to mine. Is this possible?

Only if your camcorder has an A/V input. In some countries, camcorders have A/V inputs, which means you can record from one camcorder to another in the same way as you copy from camcorder to VCR. In others, particularly those in the European Union, A/V inputs rarely feature. This is chiefly because A/V input means it can be used as a VCR, and VCRs carry a higher duty than camcorders in the EU.

Recording a friend's video by using a camcorder as a portable VCR might seem a good idea, but is only possible if your camcorder has the necessary inputs.

I have an old Betamax VCR. Can I copy on to this?

Every VCR has an input for a TV or video signal, so you can copy your videos on to any format of VCR, whether it is VHS, Betamax or Video 2000. Not all use the more standard amateur A/V connections, typically SCART or phono, but, no matter how obscure the socket used, a good electrical dealer should be able to make you up the appropriate lead.

QUALITY CONCERNS

If I buy a hi-band camcorder, will I lose any of the quality if I copy to standard VHS?

When you copy from any format to another you inevitably lose some of the picture quality. This may be particularly noticeable if you copy from hi-band to lo-band. However, the better the quality of the original, the more likely it is that the copy will be of reasonable quality – so you won't lose all the advantages of the hi-band format by copying.

When I copy my 8mm recordings of the flowers in my garden to a VHS tape in my VCR, the quality is reduced and some of the vibrancy of the colours is lost. Why is this?

Video and TV systems generally can resolve far less detail and quality than the human eye and brain. Even compared to film, video lacks vibrancy and sharpness. Copying reduces this quality further, so that your VHS copy tape will inevitably be of a poorer quality than your 8mm original. Off-air recordings should be slightly better quality than copies from 8mm to VHS, as broadcast TV systems resolve more information than lo-band formats.

 I recorded a friend's wedding on S-VHS, then copied it on to my VHS video recorder, adding music and commentary as I went along. To avoid having to add music and commentary to every copy, I would like to make copies of my VHS copy. However, although the quality is acceptable when I copy from S-VHS to VHS, when I make VHS copies of the VHS copy, the results are very poor. Is there any way of getting round this?

 There are a number of factors that determine whether a video is of acceptable quality – not least of which is your own opinion of how clear the sound and picture are.

Every time you copy, the quality is reduced, but this is most noticeable when you are copying lowlight scenes. In bright locations, such as outside the church and during the official photo shoot, the quality is fine, and may stand copying without too much resolution loss. Lowlight scenes, such as interior shots of the ceremony and the reception, may require the camcorder to boost the video gain (see Recording an Image, p. 40), and this results in a grainier image. It is scenes such as this where you notice the greatest quality loss.

A VHS copy of an S-VHS original should be fine, but a subsequent VHS copy of the copy may be unacceptable. It may be worth buying an S-VHS VCR; if you copy from S-VHS to S-VHS, subsequent VHS copies should be perfectly acceptable.

THE BASICS OF EDITING

What is editing and why is it useful?

Editing is the process of selecting which shots to include in your video. It is possible to make all the editing decisions while you are recording, effectively editing your video every time you press the camcorder's pause button. This is known as in-camera editing.

Most people start by producing home movies in this way, but soon realize that making these decisions is very difficult at the time of shooting – it is far easier to treat all of your shots as raw material from which you construct your movie later. You can then select the shots you want, determine what order you want them in, and decide how long each should last. The shots are then copied in order on to a tape in your VCR. This is known as assemble editing. You can eliminate any mistakes, such as out-of-focus

Top row: shots as first recorded; *bottom row:* the edited shots. Assemble editing teaches you to treat all your shots as raw material from which you later build your video. Here the first shot has been missed out because it is too dark. Only part of the second shot has been copied, because it was too long, and the last shot was moved to become the opening shot.

shots and shots where you were recording when you thought you had paused, and rearrange your shots into a more logical order. Assemble-edited videos are thus usually more professional-looking than videos edited in-camera.

It is a good idea to review what you have shot a number of times before you begin to assemble edit. Make a list of the usable shots, with a note of the start points. This known as logging your shots. A useful tip is to write the details of each shot on a separate index card. Note a physical description of the shot, how long it lasts and the accompanying sound. These cards can be divided into scenes – e.g. church, reception – and the cards can then be arranged into the best order. Your video then has a ready-made structure before you even begin to assemble edit it.

ASSEMBLE EDITING

When I am editing, how do I know which shots to include and which to miss out?

Each shot should be assessed on both its technical merit and its content. If the content is gripping, you can get away with substandard quality, but you should try to include only sharp, well-exposed shots with uncluttered backgrounds. Start by discarding the really awful shots – two minutes of pavement, for instance – and make out an index card for the others (see The Basics of Editing, p. 82). Once you have arranged the shots in the appropriate order, you can then review each shot again and ask: 'Does this shot contribute anything to the overall video?' The biggest problem with many videos is that they go on for too long; so if the answer is no, consider missing it out.

Include only the shots that really contribute to your video. *Above left:* this was slightly blurred and was replaced by a clearer shot. *Above right:* the soundtrack on this shot was unclear, because the subjects were too far away. *Right:* this shot was fine, so it remained.

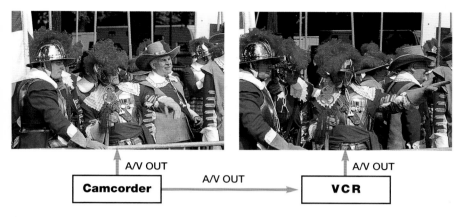

AN OUT

AN OUT

Camcorder → **VCR**

AN OUT

AN OUT

If the camcorder has two outputs, you can feed one to the VCR and one to a separate monitor.

If I have two TVs, can I monitor my camcorder tape on one and the video recorder tape on the other?

When a camcorder is connected to a VCR and the VCR is connected to a TV, the TV shows the image that is on the VCR tape if the VCR is in play or play/pause mode, but shows the camcorder image if the VCR is in record or record/pause mode and the camcorder is in play mode. Two monitors let you display the camcorder image permanently on one. You can cue and pause the camcorder tape, then cue the VCR tape, while the first monitor reminds you at exactly what point the camcorder tape was paused. If you have a hi-band camcorder, it will have two outputs – one from the S-socket and the other an A/V output. If your camcorder has only one output you can feed this to an A/V splitter – a box from which you can take two outputs.

There is always a short amount of interference between shots when I edit. Is there anything I can do about this?

Most modern video recorders feature a facility for ensuring that the edit points between shots are clean (see VCR Backspacing, p. 94). It may be that you have an old video recorder that was not designed for editing and doesn't feature this backspacing facility. If you intend to edit your videos regularly, it may be worthwhile investing in a new video recorder.

PLANNING YOUR EDITING

I feel that my videos would be more interesting if they had a structure – but where do I begin?

A movie without a structure is like words without sentences – unless you have some form of grammatical structure, it is easy to lose the thread of what is happening. The easiest way to add structure to your movie is to break it into individual scenes. Each scene should deal with a different event or subject. For instance, if you are editing the shots of a video you recorded on holiday, you can divide the shots into those that show your arrival, those that show where you are staying, and those that show you on the beach or at a site of historical interest.

A typical way of opening a scene is to show the location (1) in wide shot. We can then move closer to the action, recording the various activities (2 and 3), then end with another wide shot (4) that distances the viewer from the action.

It is much easier if you structure lots of short scenes lasting less than a minute than to plan a twenty-minute movie. A good way to open each scene is with an establishing shot – or sequence of shots. This shows you where the scene takes place and introduces the action.

Should establishing shots always be wide shots showing the location where the action is set?

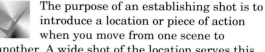

The purpose of an establishing shot is to introduce a location or piece of action when you move from one scene to another. A wide shot of the location serves this purpose well, but a pan around the location is equally good, as is a close-up, particularly if it shows writing giving the name of the location.

What are cutaways and cut-ins?

Cutaways show subjects that are related to the main action. If you were recording a sports event, for example, a cutaway might be a shot of a spectator. Cut-ins show close-ups of the main action. The shots below show a cut-in inserted between two shots of people decorating a cake. Cutaways and cut-ins are useful for condensing time. You might copy 20 seconds of the start of a race, then show a three-second cutaway of someone cheering, and then follow it with a 20-second shot of the end of the race, thus condensing the original recording.

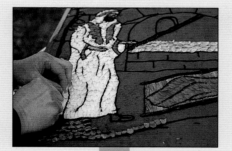

Cut-ins show close-up detail of the main action.

COMMON ERRORS

What is a jump cut and how can I avoid it?

When you edit your video – whether you edit it in-camera or assemble edit it on to your VCR – you have to be careful when you cut between two shots of the same subject. As the shots below demonstrate, if you record a few seconds of the wide shot of the two children, then pause for a few seconds before starting to record again, there will be a jump at the edit point where there is missing action. This is a jump cut, and the best way of avoiding it is to change the shot size or shooting angle between shots – for instance, cutting to the close-up of the one child. If you are assemble editing, you can avoid a jump cut by inserting a cutaway between the two similarly composed shots.

Cutting between two similarly composed shots can cause a jump cut at the edit point (*below left*). Change the shot composition between two shots of the same subject (*below right*).

When you record two people who are facing each other, make sure that you cut the shots to show one person looking from left to right and the other looking from right to left. If you use shots where they are both looking in the same direction, it will appear that they are not looking at each other at all, or that one has turned around, and your video will be confusing to watch.

What is meant by screen direction?

Subjects with eyes and moving subjects have what is known as screen direction. If they are looking or moving towards the right of the screen, their screen direction is left to right. If they are looking or moving to the left of the screen, their screen direction is right to left.

When you cut between two shots of a subject that has screen direction, be careful the screen direction doesn't change between shots. If they are looking right to left in one shot, then left to right in the subsequent shot, the viewers don't know whether they are seeing the subject from a different vantage point or whether the subject has turned round. To avoid confusion, don't cut between shots where the subject's screen direction appears to have changed. Again, a cutaway may help in this situation.

SHOT LENGTH

Is there a natural duration for a shot in video?

There isn't an ideal shot length. A shot's duration should not be judged in isolation from the shots around it. An establishing shot may need six or seven seconds for the viewer to take it in, but the same shot used later as a re-establishing shot may need only two or three.

When is the best time to end a shot?

The action in a shot should dictate shot length. If someone tells a joke that lasts 30 seconds, don't pause after 25. Ending the shot at a good edit point is more important than the actual length. As a general rule, if you

COMPLETE ACTION

CUTAWAY

INCOMPLETE ACTION

The subject matter often acts as a guide to the shot duration. If there is no action in the shot to dictate this, try the stopwatch test. Play each shot on-screen, starting a stopwatch at the start of the shot. Let your eyes roam round the shot until they come to rest, then press the stopwatch again. This gives you a rough idea of the ideal shot length. Wider shots with more information need longer on-screen than close-ups.

A shot should last long enough for the viewer to take in the information. if it lasts longer, the viewer will be distracted, and if it is shorter, they may be frustrated. *Far left:* this image may need six or seven seconds as an establishing shot, but less than half that if it is used to re-establish a location. *Middle left:* a wider shot may need several seconds for your eyes to dart around and take in all the information. *Left:* as there is only one subject in the shot, the eyes take in the whole scene in three or four seconds.

show the start of the action, show the end also. In the sequence below, starting at 1 and ending at 4 shows the whole action. Starting at 2 and running to 4 is all right, as is using shot 2 as a cutaway. But ending at shot 3 will look awkward.

ABRIDGED ACTION

PACING YOUR VIDEO

**What is meant
by 'pace'?**

The pace of a video – whether a particular sequence is fast and exciting or slow and tranquil – is largely determined by the action. But the shot length can be important too.

A video is not a photo album. Each shot has to be viewed in relation to the shots around it, and not as an individual entity in itself. In this respect, a movie is similar to a piece of music – the melody is more important than the individual notes. This is why assemble editing produces far more professional results than editing in-camera; if you don't know what shot is going to follow the shot you are recording, it is difficult to judge how long it should last on-screen.

Shot length is important because a fast cutting rate (lots of shots per minute) and irregular cutting rates (varying lengthy and short-duration shots) increase the pace. Lengthy shots and a regular cutting rhythm have the opposite effect of slowing down the pace. The conventional approach to movie-making is to match the cutting rate to the action – peaceful scenic shots have a slow, regular cutting rate, whereas in chase scenes or sporting action you should use predominantly short-duration shots, interspersed with longer shots that are full of movement.

Shot composition can affect the pace of your video too. Close-ups increase the pace, as the viewer feels more involved in the action.

Here is a classic change of pace. The first three shots (*left*) show slow action, and the shots last on-screen longer than they perhaps merit. The fourth shot (*below left*) announces a change in pace to match the train's arrival. The action is shown in close-up and the shots are shorter.

How do I change the pace of my videos, and when is it appropriate to do so?

Before you begin to assemble edit your movie – but after you have selected your shots and determined their order – think about the movie as a whole. Ask yourself where the quieter action lies, and determine where the fast action takes place. List all the sequences in your video, and give them a rating according to their pace – are they very fast, moderately fast, moderately slow, or very slow? This is your pace plan.

When you start to assemble the video, refer to the pace plan. Take a look at the rough durations you worked out for each shot based on the stop-watch test (see Shot Length, p. 90). If the sequence is a slow one, reinforce this by adding a second or so to each shot, or by evening out the shot lengths so that there is a uniform length. For the fast sequences, match the pace with the cutting rate. Cut the shot duration slightly, and increase the length of shots that include fast movement. Reaction shots and cutaways that last for only a second or so can be inserted.

VCR BACKSPACING

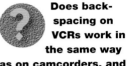

Does back-spacing on VCRs work in the same way as on camcorders, and how do I compensate for the backspace on both my camcorder and VCR?

As with camcorders, many VCRs have backspace facility to ensure clean edit points (see Backspacing, p. 46). When you press the record/pause button on your VCR, the tape rolls back slightly. This rollback can be anything from a few frames to a couple of seconds (in the diagram below we have assumed one second). When you press record to start recording the next shot, the tape rolls forward slightly to allow the VCR to lock on to the new shot's control track. In the diagram below we have assumed

VCR TAPE (SHOT 1)

Desired end of shot 1 ━━━━━━━▶

PRE-ROLL (½ SEC)

CAMCORDER TAPE (SHOT 2)

-1 sec

Play/pause tape here

-½ sec

this pre-roll to be half a second. To edit accurately, you need to work out the rollback and pre-roll times of your VCR.

To combat the inaccuracies caused by backspacing, every time you copy a shot, you should pause the VCR tape a second after the point where you want the shot to end (or whatever the appropriate time is to match your VCR's rollback time). Similarly, to ensure that the start of the new shot isn't lopped off while the VCR is pre-rolling, you should play/pause the camcorder tape half a second before the start of the new shot you want to transfer (or whatever length corresponds to your VCR's pre-roll time).

Record/pause tape here

ROLLBACK (1 SEC)

Most VCRs feature a backspacing facility to ensure that there is no interference at the edit points. As a result of this, the start and end of each shot will be lopped off unless you compensate for it. You can do this by pausing the VCR tape after the point where you want the previous shot to end, and then starting the camcorder tape before the point at which you want the shot to start.

Desired start of shot 2

0 sec   ½ sec   1 sec

SYNCHRO-EDIT

Why do some people use two VCRs for editing? Do VCRs make better playback machines than camcorders?

Good edit VCRs have controls that are less delicate than camcorder controls, and feature tape transport controls that are easier to use. Many also have jog/shuttle dials that can advance the tape frame by frame.

Hi8 (*right*) and S-VHS decks are best for editing.

Having to release the camcorder and VCR pause buttons at the same time can be tricky. Is there a way of making this easier?

Some manufacturers have come up with a simple way of semi-automating the editing process. They sell synchro-edit leads that connect between the playback and record machines. These enable you to control both units through one set of controls (as the signal is passed along the lead). With some systems you use the camcorder's controls, with others, the VCR's.

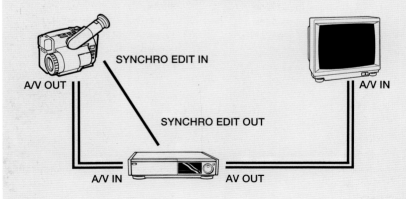

SYNCHRO EDIT IN

A/V OUT

A/V IN

SYNCHRO EDIT OUT

A/V IN

AV OUT

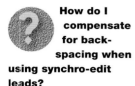

How do I compensate for back-spacing when using synchro-edit leads?

Synchro-editing should take care of this accuracy problem too. Some companies build a delay into their synchro-edit leads so that they compensate for the VCR's backspacing. You should test the accuracy of your leads before you start using them to edit. It may be that you still have to compensate manually, as the delay may not be entirely accurate. But generally synchro-edit leads are extremely accurate – rarely out by more than a few frames. Such small delays – usually less than a quarter of a second – are rarely a problem.

With synchro-edit, a delay is built in to compensate for the backspacing. If your system is accurate, the end and start points of the shots should be as you desire without your having to pause the VCR tape after the required point.

Are synchro-edit leads compatible between manufacturers?

Unfortunately not. Canon and Sanyo use the Sony system, but JVC uses an incompatible system. Panasonic's is incompatible with both. You also need a camcorder and VCR that both feature a dedicated synchro-edit socket.

EDIT CONTROLLERS

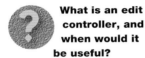

What is an edit controller, and when would it be useful?

 If you have several hundred shots to copy, physically cueing the tape for each shot can be time-consuming. Edit controllers (above) automate this process. They connect to the VCR and camcorder (see below) and duplicate the transport functions of both machines. Some also store dozens of start and end points. Programme in the edit points as you watch the playback and press 'assemble'. The editor automatically assembles the video.

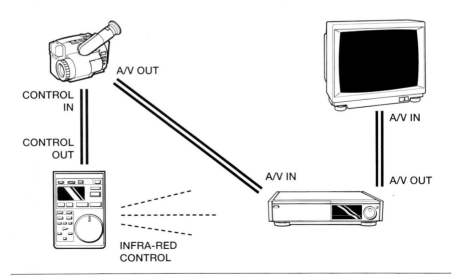

A/V OUT

CONTROL IN

CONTROL OUT

A/V IN

A/V IN

A/V OUT

INFRA-RED CONTROL

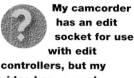

My camcorder has an edit socket for use with edit controllers, but my video has no such socket. Does this mean I need a new VCR?

Not necessarily. An edit controller is a versatile tool that can control your VCR's tape transport functions without an edit socket. It needs a hard-wire connection with the camcorder, because it has to control its play, pause, rewind and fast forward functions and read its tape counter to know when to start and stop each shot. This information is carried through the camcorder's edit socket to the edit controller. But the edit controller doesn't need to read the VCR's counter information, so you can simply control the VCR with infra-red remote control. Any remote-control VCR can be controlled in this way.

How do edit controllers assemble edit automatically?

First you have to programme the counter information for the start and end points of each shot into the editor. Most editors run a test to work out the VCR's backspace time. They are not necessarily more accurate than synchro-editing, but they shouldn't be seconds out.

0:16:23

0:16:31

0:16:44

0:16:49

TIME-CODE EDITING

`0:13:21:06`

What is a time-code?

Time-code is a system that labels every frame of your video individually. The advantage of this is that, if you have an editor that can read the time-code information, it uses this rather than the counter information to cue the camcorder tape during assemble editing. This should then guarantee frame accuracy rather than accuracy within a few frames.

Can I add time-code to my tapes after they have been recorded?

Domestic hardware uses one of two time-code editing systems. These are RCTC (rewritable consumer time-code) and VITC (vertically integrated time-code). RCTC is associated with 8mm equipment and VITC with VHS. Both can be added at the time of recording or while copying to another tape, if your camcorder is suitably equipped, but RCTC can also be added later without affecting the existing sound, picture or control information.

What equipment do I need to time-code edit?

 Ideally, you should have a camcorder with time-code writing ability (see below). Some VHS camcorders don't have VITC built in, but they will take an add-on time-code generator. A suitably equipped editor is needed also, to read the information. These can often add time-code too, so you can add it to your tapes even if your camcorder has no such facility.

 I have an RCTC editor and I recently went back through some of my old tapes and added time-code. When I came to edit them, I found that although some of the scenes were fine, some of them were from completely different parts of the tape. Is it likely that my time-code writer is faulty?

 It is possible that your time-code editor is not writing properly, but this is not necessarily the case. RCTC needs an uninterrupted control track to lay down the time-code successfully. For instance, if you leave a blank minute of unrecorded tape before your video begins, the writer will not start adding time-code until it detects the first control signal.

What this means is that if your camcorder tape does not feature continuous recordings – for instance, if there are any blank spots of tape in the middle – the editor will stop writing the time-code at this point. As soon as it encounters a new control track, it will begin writing again from 0. There will thus be more than one frame on the tape with the same identity number. This accounts for the fact that while some of the edited scenes are correct, there are incorrect edits where the editor has chosen the correct time-code information but the wrong shot.

USING TIME-CODE

When would time-code be most useful?

For most situations, an error of a few frames in cutting accuracy won't make a great deal of difference. If you are showing a montage of images from an event or a sequence of location shots to give the feel of an area, half a second added to or taken from the end of each shot won't matter at all.

When you are directing the action, however, accuracy is vital. Shots that contain people talking, for instance, must have completely accurate edit points. Imagine you are recording two people having a conversation. You record a shot of one of them saying something, pause the camcorder, then record a shot of the second person replying. If even a few frames are cut off, you may miss the end of the sentence. If a few frames are added, there will be an awkward pause between the two sentences.

What do the terms 'cutting on action' and 'cutting on the turn' mean?

 If you cut between two shots of the same subject, it is easy to disguise the cut if you cut 'on action', or mid-action. Record the person performing the same action twice, first from one camera angle, then from a second. When you edit the shots together, cut halfway through the action. In the shots below, for instance, the cut comes as the subject turns his head. You have to be careful that the first shot ends at exactly the same point in the action as the second begins – otherwise there is either double or missing action.

Cutting on the turn is a similar technique used for 'talking to camera' shots. The speaker delivers a couple of sentences, turns, delivers a couple more, turns back and so on. After each turn, pause the camcorder and move to another position. Ask them to repeat the turn and cut the shots together so the edit point is in the middle of the turn. The person has to remember only a few sentences at a time, but it looks like they are delivering a continuous monologue.

Cutting on action helps disguise the edit point, but you have to make sure you end the first shot at exactly the same point as you start the second.

INSERT EDITING

How does insert edit work on a video recorder?

Video recorders backspace to line up the control pulses of the old track with the control pulses of the new (see VCR Backspacing, p. 94), thus ensuring there is a clean edit point between the two shots. As with camcorder insert edit, you don't re-record the control track, only the video (and hi-fi stereo audio if the VCR has this).

With VCR insert edit, you can change the pace of your videos after you have recorded them by

HI-FI SOUNDTRACK

PICTURE

LINEAR MONO SOUND

CONTROL PULSE ●

inserting fast shots over existing footage to increase the shot rate. Some VCRs have insert-edit functions that work in the same way as record – you simply press insert/pause instead of record/pause. Others work in combination with the VCR's tape counter. Decide where you want the inserted shot to end and set the tape counter to zero at that point. Wind back to where you want the insert to start and begin inserting the shot. The VCR automatically stops recording when it reaches zero. Probably the best use of insert edit is in combination with assemble edit. Assemble the video first, then use insert edit to insert reaction shots and cutaways.

NEW HI-FI SOUNDTRACK

Inserting a cutaway is a lot easier with insert edit than with assemble editing. Rather than having to record three separate shots – one of the girl on the fairground ride, one of the spectator, and one of the girl again – insert edit allows you to record the girl first, then insert the spectator in the middle of the shot – and you don't even have to worry about backspacing.

Can I insert edit both picture and sound over a shot without affecting the sound of the original shot – or can I insert new video only?

When you insert edit, not only is the control track not re-recorded, but the VHS linear mono track is also left untouched, so the sound of the original shot accompanies the insert. If the VCR is mono, no new sound is recorded. If it is hi-fi stereo, new sound is recorded on the hi-fi tracks, so you get a combination of new and original sound.

If you don't want to record new sound with the insert, don't connect the audio leads between the camcorder and VCR when you copy. If you want to make copies of your edited video, the VCR may let you select whether you want to output sound from the hi-fi tracks, the linear track, or both.

WORKING WITH INSERTS

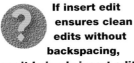 **If insert edit ensures clean edits without backspacing, can't I simply insert edit instead of assembling?**

This is possible, but cueing the end of each shot before you insert it and rewinding to the desired point may be more time-consuming. However, if you can insert as easily as you can record, there is no reason why not – but you will not record on the linear track, which is available for audio dubbing.

Also you cannot insert edit unless the tape has a control track. To lay a control track on a blank VCR tape, put the camcorder in record mode, but leave the lens cap on. Connect it to the VCR and press the VCR's record button. This is known as 'blacking' the tape.

CONTROL PULSE ●

SOUND: CONTINUOUS MUSIC FROM MASTER SHOT (LEFT)

PICTURE

Can I use insert edit to lay individual shots over a pre-recorded piece of music or continuous soundtrack?

This is a common professional technique that works well with home movies too.

First black the tape, then rewind it and audio dub the desired piece of music – this appears on the linear mono track only. The next stage is to insert edit various shots over the music. The advantage of performing the operation this way round (rather than laying the video down first) is that you can time the start and end points of the

If I have a mono video recorder, is it possible only to insert edit video without recording over the control track – or can I add sound to the mono track at the same time?

There are three ways of laying information on the tape. First is record, which records over the control track, video, hi-fi stereo (if available) and linear mono. Second is insert edit, which re-records over the video (and hi-fi stereo) only; and third is audio dub, which records over the linear mono track only.

If you want to simultaneously copy sound and vision on to a blacked tape in a mono VCR with insert edit, press the insert-edit and audio-dub buttons at the same time. However, unless the sound and picture are simultaneous (such as with speech), there is no reason why you can't insert edit and audio dub at different times. If the sound is simultaneous, then it may be as well to assemble the shot, rather than insert edit.

shots to coincide with changes in the musical tempo. A variation (as illustrated in the sequence of pictures above) is to record a live piece of music in continuous wide shot (above left) and lay this on the tape. Then go back and insert lots of cutaways of close-ups over the master shot. Unless you show an instrument that is obviously not playing at the time, the viewers won't notice whether or not the action matches the music.

PROCESSORS

**What are
processors
and what can
they do?**

Processing units allow you to manipulate
the video signal. They cannot take a bad
image and make it good – you can't, for
instance, add detail where there isn't detail, or
sharpen an out of focus image – but processors do
offer basic enhancements that help retain quality
during the copying process. Many also offer
colour manipulation and special effects.

**What are the
important
features on a
processor and
what do they do?**

The basic processing functions tweak the
picture in various ways. Names of
controls vary, but most camcorders have
facilities like the ones you'd find on a TV, such
as colour and contrast adjustments. Detail or
sharpness controls can soften harsh images and
harden up soft edges. A colour control boosts or
decreases the overall colour level, but more
useful are individual colour-manipulation

My enhancer has no S-input. Will it still work if I upgrade to an S-VHS camcorder?

Your enhancer is not designed for hi-band equipment. Besides, neither S-VHS nor Hi8 should need enhancing, particularly if your video was recorded in reasonable light. If you want to take advantage of the signal-processing functions, you will need a processor with S-input if you want to retain the quality.

I have a PAL TV, and I find strong reds often bleed to the right of the picture, appearing to smear. Will an enhancer help?

Unfortunately, it probably won't. You are unlikely to have either a camcorder or a tape problem. The problem more likely lies with the PAL TV system itself. With this TV standard, there is a slow fall-off of the electrical signal. As the TV scans from left to right, this can cause smearing towards the right. Some newer TVs feature circuitry to prevent this. If you are looking for a new TV, look for models with systems such as CTI (colour transient improvement).

controls, for the red, green and blue parts of the signal. By altering their relative strengths, you can correct faulty colour balance as well as manipulate the image in more subtle ways. The images below show the same scene, but the one on the right is slightly bluer. By reducing the blue part of the signal you can make a cool day seem a lot warmer, and by increasing the blue, make a warm day seem colder.

These scenes were shot in the same conditions, but by increasing the blue part of the signal, the picture on the right has been made to look as if it were shot on a colder day.

USING PROCESSORS

I use a number of units in my editing set-up – a processor, a sound mixer and an editor. As they are daisy-chained together, is there any particular order in which I should connect them?

If the video signal doesn't have to pass through your edit controller, its position in the set-up is irrelevant as far as the processor is concerned. But if you have a number of units that affect the picture – such as titling units and processors – you should always place the processor closest to the video recorder in the chain. If you don't, you might find yourself processing or manipulating a signal that gets further degraded before it is recorded by your video recorder.

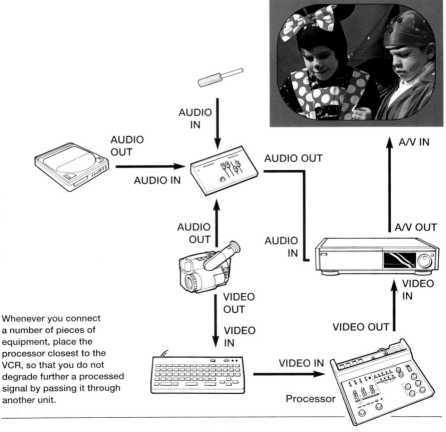

AUDIO IN

AUDIO OUT

AUDIO IN

AUDIO OUT

A/V IN

AUDIO IN

A/V OUT

AUDIO OUT

AUDIO IN

VIDEO OUT

VIDEO IN

VIDEO IN

VIDEO OUT

VIDEO IN

Whenever you connect a number of pieces of equipment, place the processor closest to the VCR, so that you do not degrade further a processed signal by passing it through another unit.

Processor

My friend and I took pictures at a steam rally. However, when we edited them together, we found the colours were slightly different. In my shots, the reds were distinctly more pink. Is there anything I can do?

 If the colour of one of the camcorders is distinctly washed out or has a significant colour cast, then there may be a fault in the colour-balance or signal-processing circuitry. If it is still under warranty, take it back to be checked. Otherwise, manipulating the colour signal using a processor should help. Try altering the weaker signal to boost it to the level of the stronger one.

Be careful when videoing steam engines – noxious fumes can dirty your video heads.

 If your camcorder has a different colour bias from another, there may be a fault in the colour-balance circuitry. A processor may help to correct this.

 What is a time-base corrector and when is it useful?

A time-base corrector is a device that generates new control pulses to replace existing signals that may be weak or degraded. Strong control pulses are necessary for some computer video applications, but they also help improve vertical lines in the scene.

SPECIAL EFFECTS

I have seen some processors that claim to offer various 'special effects'. What are these, and when are they useful?

Some video processors, special-effects generators and computer video programs can be used to create special effects in your videos. Some effects are very obvious and are particularly suited for movies you are directing yourself – such as comedy or science fiction stories. In other circumstances, special effects should be used sparingly – they will lose their impact if overused. Other effects are more subtle and are used to create a certain mood. Some processors also have titling units, faders and audio mixers built in.

Inserts title over split screen

If the processor has a titling facility built in, you can have a video image on half the screen and opening or closing credits on the other half of the screen.

A matte is any shape that blocks off part of the screen. With processors, the matte is usually a single colour. You can choose which side of the matte you want the video to occupy and which part should be plain coloured.

By subtly manipulating colour controls and contrast, you can create a sinister or moody world. Here, the blues have been boosted, the contrast increased and the brightness reduced slightly. The result is far more atmospheric than the regular-coloured original.

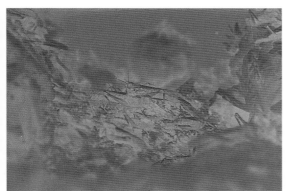

One of the most bizarre effects is the positive/negative function, which renders each area of the screen the opposite colour to reality. Here, macro makes the locusts in the shots appear larger than they are, while the pos/neg button creates an other-world feel.

Various effects that are suited to pop videos, such as mosaic and multi-imaging, are found on special-effects generators – especially those that are computer-based. In a normal video, such an effect would probably be too much, but with music videos, anything goes.

TRICK PLAY

I have seen video recorders advertised with trick play facility. What is trick play?

Trick play is the term given to playing back your tape backwards or at any speed other than the regular speed at which it was originally recorded.

Trick play is another reason why video recorders make more suitable playback machines than camcorders. Some camcorders offer slow-motion playback, but video recorders with clean fast- and slow-motion playback are more widely available and can be controlled with the jog/shuttle control. Some models give cleaner trick play than others, with some only offering fast playback with unsightly horizontal bars across the screen.

Freezeframe – where a still image is held on-screen – is also a form of trick play. Freezeframes can be used at the end of a video – or at least at the end of a sequence – and should show dramatic or interesting action.

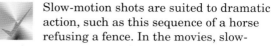

When would I want slow-motion playback and would I be able to retain slow sound?

Slow-motion shots are suited to dramatic action, such as this sequence of a horse refusing a fence. In the movies, slow-motion sequences are often reserved for high-impact moments that last for a short amount of time, such as crossing the finish line of a race, throwing a punch, or someone being shot. If you know you want to show a particular sequence in slow motion, record it with a fast shutter so that the action doesn't blur. In all but a few top-end or pro VCRs, the sound is lost in slow motion.

Although the action here is quite dramatic, in reality it lasted only a very short amount of time. You could heighten the drama of the moment by playing the shot back in slow motion. A fast shutter ensured that the subject didn't blur through movement.

FADES

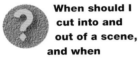

When should I cut into and out of a scene, and when should I use a fade?

Below: The fade out/fade in can be used to suggest the passage of time. We see the animal going about its business in the first shot, then the next interesting shot we have of it took place some time later. The fade out/in tells the viewers they are not watching continuous action.

The most basic way of moving from one shot to another (called 'transition') is the cut. This is when one shot ends at full sound and picture intensity and the next follows immediately afterwards. Use this in most circumstances, and use more advanced transitions when they are justified.

The fade is the next easiest transition to perform. Some camcorders have fade buttons built in, and a lot of processors feature fade as an option. There are two kinds of fade – the fade out and the fade in. With the fade out, the picture is slowly faded to a blank screen and the sound is faded down. The fade in is the opposite – the screen slowly fades in from blank to full intensity, while the sound simultaneously gets louder.

The most useful feature of fades is that they can alter the pace of the action. If you cut to a

Opposite page: Fading out is a good way of ending a sequence. Fading slows the pace and suggests the end of a particular event. If the next scene shows lively action, you should cut in. If it shows the slow start of a day, fade in.

Below, top row: Fading in creates a gentle introduction to a scene. It indicates immediately that time has elapsed since the last shot.

blank screen, then fade in to the next shot, the fast pace will abruptly cease, no matter how much fast action there was in the previous sequence. Fading out from a scene then cutting into the next can increase the pace, particularly if you cut into a close-up or a scene with a loud soundtrack. It is best to fade out from and fade in to slow shots – it looks odd if you fade out from a fast shot such as a car racing round a circuit.

You can fade out of one scene and fade in to the next, and this can have various effects. The most significant is to suggest the passage of time, such as fading out from a location at night and in to the next shot to show it is the following morning. In some TV dramas, however, the convention has grown up to use the fade out/in as a dramatic pause; at the point of highest drama in the scene (the villain pulls a gun on the hero) the picture fades out then fades back in again. The scene is identical, and the fade out/in has simply acted as a way of prolonging the dramatic moment.

ADVANCED TRANSITIONS

**What is a
vision mixer?**

 A vision mixer is any unit that can combine two or more video signals and show them on-screen at the same time. Its most obvious use is to enable you to perform a 'mix' or 'dissolve'. This is when one shot fades out as another is faded in. Halfway through the mix, both shots are on the screen at equal intensity.

The dissolve is usually controlled by a sliding lever. If it is positioned at one end of the slide, the shot from one input is shown on the screen at full intensity, if at the other end, the other shot is shown. You can perform the dissolve manually, by sliding the lever as quickly or as slowly as you like, but some units (as well as computer software) allow you to programme the length of the dissolve and press an auto button. The mixer then carries out the transition automatically. Dissolves slow the pace of the video – the longer the dissolve, the slower the pace.

**When should
I use a
dissolve?**

 The dissolve is a softer transition than the cut. It suggests that action has moved on slightly, so it can be used as a way of avoiding jump cuts when you cut between two similarly composed shots of the same subject. This is sloppy, however, and you should really avoid jump cuts by recomposing. Dissolves can be used in a montage sequence to suggest action is

What other advanced transitions can I produce with a vision mixer?

Even the most basic vision mixer can perform a wipe, which is where one shot replaces another by wiping over it. There are hundreds of wipe patterns to choose from. With the most basic, a line starts at one edge, then wipes vertically, horizontally or diagonally across the frame. Wipes can easily look hackneyed, so beware of overdoing them.

This is a more advanced wipe pattern – the circular (or iris) wipe. The shot of the child started off as a tiny dot in the centre of the first shot, then wiped out until it filled the screen.

being missed out and that only the significant bits are being shown. You could, for instance, dissolve between a dozen shots of someone cooking a meal, each one taking place several minutes later. If you were to cut, the action would jump at the edit points. Like fades out/in, dissolves can be used when you want to slow the action right down.

Dissolves create a slow, restful pace, perfectly suited to montage sequences of restful subjects, such as flowers.

TITLING

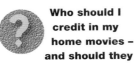

Who should I credit in my home movies – and should they come at the start or the end of the video?

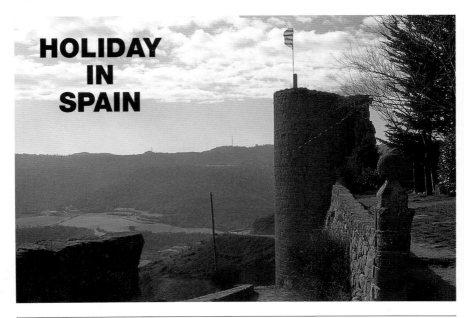

Professional movies have such extensive credits because movie-makers are contractually obliged to include all those people. If you include credits in an amateur movie, it is entirely up to you who you mention. Put only the important names (such as yourself) at the beginning, but don't credit every single job you performed. Even if you did everything, just stick to a couple of good ones – such as producer, director or writer.

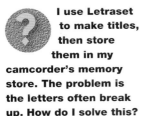

I use Letraset to make titles, then store them in my camcorder's memory store. The problem is the letters often break up. How do I solve this?

Camcorder digital title stores have a very limited memory capacity. This means they will not be able to store the detailed information required for complicated typefaces. Stick to large, bold lettering, avoiding the edges of the screen, as the titles will distort. They also look neater if they are not falling off the edge of the screen.

HOLIDAY IN SPAIN

How do I make my titles scroll up or across the screen?

Some titling units allow you to scroll your titles, but you can make your own scroller out of a couple of rolling pins or cardboard tubes with a long sheet of paper attached between them. Manually focus the camcorder and set it on a tripod, then slowly scroll the paper up past the camcorder's lens. The result should be professionally scrolled credits.

TITLES CAN BE SCROLLED UP TO MAKE THEM LOOK MORE PROFESSIONAL

What are the advantages of using dedicated titling units and titlers built into mixers and processors?

The more sophisticated the equipment (or the computer software), the more you are likely to be able to produce creative or animated titles. The simple titling systems built into camcorders are very basic by comparison.

Individual letters in a title can be animated when you use more sophisticated titling equipment.

AUDIO DUBBING

I would like to audio-dub my videotapes. What equipment am I going to need?

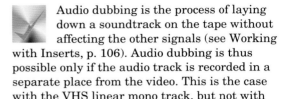

Audio dubbing is the process of laying down a soundtrack on the tape without affecting the other signals (see Working with Inserts, p. 106). Audio dubbing is thus possible only if the audio track is recorded in a separate place from the video. This is the case with the VHS linear mono track, but not with VHS hi-fi stereo or 8mm FM mono or stereo.

Some top-end Hi8 camcorders boast digital stereo PCM soundtracks as well as the standard FM soundtrack. This is semi-independent of the rest of the signals. As with VHS linear mono, you can dub on to the PCM soundtrack. But you cannot insert edit on to the video and FM soundtracks without affecting the PCM track. If you want to audio dub but have an 8mm camcorder, edit your videos on to VHS and audio dub on to the VHS VCR.

AUDIO-DUBBED COMMENTARY OR MUSIC

When is audio dub most useful?

Audio dub is most useful when the existing soundtrack is uninteresting or non-existent. You can then eliminate the original sound completely and audio dub music or commentary over the whole sequence. The art of good editing is to play down the edit points, rather than drawing attention to them, just as

My VCR doesn't have audio dub. But can't I achieve the same result by connecting my music system to the audio in, but not connecting anything to the video in?

Unfortunately, that won't work. When you press the hi-fi record button, you record on to all parts of the tape – the video, audio and control track. If you don't connect anything to the video track but simply connect your hi-fi system to the VCR's audio-in socket, you will still record over the existing video, but you won't record anything that is watchable – all you will get is interference and picture noise.

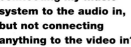

I recently travelled from the UK to Australia. Although both countries are PAL, when I tried to dub from my 8mm to a VHS video recorder, I got the picture, but not the sound. Why is this?

Although the UK and Australia both use the PAL TV standard, the two sound transmission systems are different. However, this should be a problem only if you are connecting your camcorder to an Australian VCR via the RF (aerial) socket. Were you to connect the camcorder's audio out to the VCR's audio in socket, rather than the aerial socket, the sound would have recorded as normal. This problem occurs with other TV standards too.

when you read a good story, you shouldn't notice the punctuation. One of the best ways of smoothing transitions between shots is to have a continuous soundtrack, which is possible with audio dub. If you have a hi-fi VCR, you can retain the original sound on the hi-fi stereo soundtracks, mixing it with the dubbed track.

SOUND MIXING

How do I add commentary and music to my videos once they have been edited?

The trick to sound mixing is to add music, commentary and so forth without copying so much that you degrade the picture quality. If your VCR has audio-dub facility, you can add music and commentary without losing further quality after the first edit stage.

VCR 1

RECORD

Tape: Original material

Tape: Edit master

1. First, edit your video in the normal way by copying from your camcorder (or playback VCR) to a tape in your video recorder. This edited copy is your edit master.

VCR 1

VCR 2

RECORD

Tape: Edit master

Sound mixer

Tape: Sound master

2. Copy your edited video to a second VCR. Connect the VCR's audio out to one of the inputs of an audio mixer. A music system and microphone can be connected to other audio mixer inputs. Volume sliders by each of the inputs enable you to set the correct relative volumes. This is your sound master.

VCR 2

VCR 1

AUDIO DUB ONLY

Tape: Sound master

Tape: Edit master with mixed sound

3. Using audio dub, copy the sound master back on to the edit master. You will then have the mixed soundtrack on the original edited tape, so you will not even have lost one further generation of picture quality.

LIVE SOUND OR ANIMAL SOUND EFFECTS

COMMENTARY

CONTINUOUS MUSIC

LIVE SOUND OR ANIMAL SOUND EFFECTS

COMMENTARY

CONTINUOUS MUSIC

Neither my camcorder nor my VCR has audio-dub facility. Is there any other way of adding music to my videos after I have shot them?

If you are not editing your videos but are simply copying what you have shot from your camcorder tape to your VCR tape, you can add music or commentary while copying. Connect the camcorder's video out to the video in on the VCR, and connect the video's audio out to one input of a sound mixer. A microphone is attached to a second input, and you simply talk or play music while the tape is being copied. If you want to edit your videos, you will have to edit first, then copy the edited version, adding sound at this point. Of course, the picture quality suffers when it is copied a second time.

COMMENTARY TIPS

What is the best way of writing a commentary?

Make the commentary sound informal – it should be natural and conversational, not stilted. You don't have to talk over every frame – your commentary should add information, not simply state what is on-screen. The viewers can see this for themselves.

It may be best to talk over the less exciting moments, so your commentary doesn't compete for attention with the action. The important words in the commentary should come at the edit point at the start of the shot. The pictures below demonstrate how.

'Everybody gathered in the village for the 150th annual well-dressing, the highlight of which was...'

'...the crowning of the May Queen.'

 **I recently edited a copy of a video I took on holiday and later audio dubbed a commentary. I sent the tape to a friend I met on holiday, but before doing so I made a copy of the edited tape. He claims his copy contains just commentary, yet mine has both commentary and the original sound.**

 This is entirely possible. You audio dubbed a commentary on to the linear mono edge track of your videotape. The sound was initially recorded on to your hi-fi tracks and your linear track. The edit master that you sent to your friend has the original sound on the hi-fi tracks and the commentary on the linear mono track. If he has a hi-fi video recorder, he will hear both original sound and commentary. But if, as seems likely, he has a mono VCR, it won't be able to play back the hi-fi tracks, so it will play only what is on the linear mono track – the commentary. The copy you made will have all the sound on all three tracks.

 I have a mono camcorder with audio-dub facility. Is it possible to add commentary to some of the sports matches I shoot without losing the original sound? Or will I have to copy the whole tape to my video recorder, losing a generation of video quality in the process?

 If you had a stereo VHS-C camcorder, this would be no problem – you could simply dub on to the linear mono track. With a mono camcorder it is still possible, using a method similar to that for mixing sound described on p. 124. You have to copy your video to a VCR tape, adding the commentary at this point by connecting the original sound to one input of an audio mixer, and adding your commentary via a microphone connected to another input. Once you have created this 'sound master', you can audio dub the combined commentary back on to your camcorder tape. Not all machines run at identical speeds, however, so it is possible that the original sound will become out of sync after a while.

MUSIC AND WILDTRACKS

 I recorded my friend's wedding in a church, but there is a lot of echo on the soundtrack – is there anything I can do about it now?

 Unfortunately there is very little you can do about this with domestic equipment. Some hi-fi systems have digital signal processing chips that generally increase the echo to simulate different environments – such as a cathedral. Although there are ways of making sound played in your living-room sound as if it were in a church, nobody has yet invented a system that makes a recording in a church sound as if it is in your living-room.

 Can I attach my hi-fi system to my camcorder using the camcorder's microphone socket?

 While this is possible, it will result in a considerable amount of sound distortion. You can counter this by connecting through the line input of a mixer microphone, or by using a special connection lead that will match the impedence of the audio to that of the microphone. Consult a dealer to obtain the correct lead.

Am I breaking copyright if I dub music or sound effects on to my videos?

You don't need to worry too much about copyright if your video is strictly for home viewing, although copyright-free music is available – look at ads in video magazines. There are two forms of copyright to worry about – that on the music itself (if the composer has been dead for more than 50 years it is copyright-free) and that on the recording. Dedicated sound-effects CDs (below) are copyright-free.

What is a wildtrack?

A wildtrack is a piece of continuous sound that is recorded on to a video to add atmosphere and help to retain the continuity when there are lots of visual cuts.

For example, if you were making a video about wildlife in your area, you could record uninterrupted woodland sounds and then dub this soundtrack on to your tape in the same way as you might add music or commentary.

SYNC SOUND

WILDTRACK: CONTINUOUS WOODLAND NOISE

VIDEO STILLS

 How can I transfer a still photograph to video?

 There are a number of methods of transferring stills to video, the simplest of which is to record the still photograph through the lens. The print has to be evenly lit, so that the exposure is good but so that there aren't any reflective highlights. A lamp angled at 45° to the picture surface is best. It will illuminate the print, but the bounced light from the surface of the print will be reflected away from the camcorder's lens.

Two lamps, positioned either side of the print, but both aimed down at a 45°angle, are even better. Other transfer methods are available, such as dedicated slide- or negative-to-video transfer attachments.

It is possible to convert slides and transparencies to video by still recording the image. It is essential that the print is evenly lit, as shown here, and that there is no reflection off the surface.

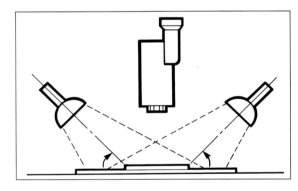

 What is Photo CD?

 Photo CD is a method of converting your prints or slides to electronic video images. The operation is performed at a processing lab and the images are stored on gold-coloured compact discs.

The images have to be played back through a Photo CD player, so you would have to purchase one to make use of this method. The Photo CD player also doubles as a normal audio CD player, and it has a video out, so that the images can be recorded directly on to your VCR.

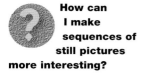

**How can
I make
sequences of
still pictures
more interesting?**

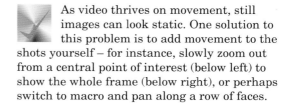

As video thrives on movement, still images can look static. One solution to this problem is to add movement to the shots yourself – for instance, slowly zoom out from a central point of interest (below left) to show the whole frame (below right), or perhaps switch to macro and pan along a row of faces.

**What is still
video?**

Still video is a system that creates video images by using a dedicated camera that records electronic images directly, rather than recording photos on to film. Still-video cameras have video outputs, so each still can be transferred directly on to tape. Current models store images on floppy disk. Still-video cameras are costly compared to 35mm compact cameras, but the cheapest sell for less than any camcorder. Quality is poorer than film, but good for video.

Still-video cameras come in a range of models and store video images on floppy disks and have video outputs so pictures can be played directly on your VCR.

CINE TO VIDEO TRANSFER

 When I try to project old cine films of my children on to a wall so I can video them, the pictures often look fuzzy. What can I do to improve this?

Project on to a small area to prevent cine footage from looking too fuzzy.

 To begin with, set the focus of both the camcorder and the projector manually – this way you can guarantee that both units are properly focused. Place them as square as possible to each other, side by side or one above the other if possible. Use a small projection area, as quality degrades with larger projection.

 When I transfer cine to my camcorder, the colours look washed out. Is there anything I can do about this?

You may have a white-balance problem, or the old footage may simply have faded or been overexposed slightly at the time of shooting. You may be able to add a bit of colour by connecting the camcorder directly to your VCR and recording directly on to a VCR tape. This way you can place a processing unit in between and boost the colour saturation as you record.

It may also be that your camcorder is not setting the correct colour balance. To ensure correct white balance, turn the lights off in the room and run the cine projector without film in it on to a white wall or screen. If your camcorder allows, lock the white balance at this reading. You will also get a more saturated projection image when the projector is close to the screen, so try moving the projector and the camcorder closer to the wall.

When I use a tele-cine to video converter, there is a bright spot on the centre of the image. Is it possible to get rid of this?

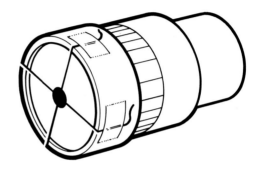

This is caused by the bulb in the centre of the projector creating a brighter segment of the image in the centre of the frame. The only solution is to mask off the centre of the image – perhaps by suspending a circular piece of card over the centre of the projection lens. As the card will be completely out of focus, you will not see the circle – the amount of light from the centre of the image will simply be reduced.

A piece of card suspended over the centre of the projector lens helps eliminate the hotspot caused by the projector bulb.

How can I deaden the sound of the projector on the video soundtrack?

Obviously, the further you are away from the projector, the less motor noise will be picked up by the camcorder. If your cine footage contains no sound, simply disable the camcorder's microphone by connecting an external microphone to the microphone socket and leaving the microphone switched off. If your projector has an audio output, connect the audio directly to the camcorder's microphone socket (see, however, p. 128). Alternatively, connect the audio directly to a VCR's audio input and record on to that.

The videos I have recorded from cine seem to flicker – can I do anything about this?

Flicker is natural, as the projector and your camcorder are running at different frame rates. Don't set a high-speed shutter, as this may result in the image strobing, which accentuates the effect. If the projector has a variable speed control, try altering this until the effect is minimized.

Glossary

AGC (automatic gain control) The purpose of AGC is to ensure correct exposure by varying the current supplied to (and therefore the sensitivity of) the image-recording CCD. Increasing the current is known as 'boosting the gain', and this happens automatically in low light conditions unless your camcorder allows manual exposure, AGC lock or has a program mode such as twilight mode.

ALC (automatic level control) Audio equivalent of AGC, boosting the sensitivity of the microphone in quiet conditions. Boosting the sound level increases hiss and sensitivity to camcorder handling noise. Can be overridden only if your camcorder has manual level controls.

Aspect ratio The relationship between the width of a picture and its height. Conventional TV screens have a 4:3 ratio (four wide to three high). A widescreen TV has a ratio of 16:9.

Assemble editing Process whereby shots recorded by your camcorder are copied individually on to a tape in a video recorder. Assemble editing allows you to miss out, shorten or rearrange shots.

Audio dubbing Replacing the existing sound (or part of the existing sound) with a new soundtrack. Particularly useful for adding music, commentary or sound effects. On mono VHS camcorders and VCRs with audio-dub facility, audio dubbing replaces the entire original soundtrack, whereas on hi-fi stereo models, it replaces the mono soundtrack only and leaves the stereo tracks untouched. Possible only on 8mm and Hi8 camcorders that feature PCM digital audio. Audio dubbing can also be performed when you copy from one tape to another.

Audio mixer Device for mixing sounds from several sources, such as a microphone, hi-fi system and sound from the camcorder tape. Each sound source plugs into a different input and the combined output is recorded on to a new tape. Individual level controls for each input enable you to balance the various sound sources.

Autofocus (AF) Various systems for ensuring the subject is sharp. Systems can be either active or passive. Active systems send out an infra-red beam and measure the amount of time it takes to bounce off the subject and return to the camcorder. Passive systems work on the principle that subjects have the greatest contrast when they are in focus.

Backlight compensation (BLC) When light comes from behind the subject, the camcorder's exposure system detects the light and closes the iris in an attempt to expose the subject correctly. This can cause the subject to be underexposed – or in extreme circumstances, silhouetted. Some camcorders feature a backlight compensation (BLC) button that when pressed opens the iris wider than the setting selected by the camcorder's autoexposure system. Some camcorders have automatic backlight compensation built in.

Backspacing When an audio/video signal is recorded on to videotape, a control track is recorded too. This is a series of regularly-spaced electronic pulses that keeps the playback heads correctly aligned. When you record a new shot, the new control pulses have to match the old. To do this, the camcorder rewinds the tape slightly when you press record/pause button. The control pulses from the two shots are now correctly aligned, but the end of the previous shot is recorded over.

Battery discharger NiCad batteries give less running time if they are recharged without first being almost fully discharged. This reduction in running time is known as memory effect. Dischargers discharge rechargeable batteries. Chargers often have dischargers built in, trickling away the battery's charge before recharging it again. This eliminates any chance of the battery suffering from memory effect.

Blacking Process of laying a control track on a tape without recording an audio or video signal by recording with the lens cap on. This allows you to audio dub or insert edit on to the tape without using the record button.

BNC Type of A/V connector sometimes found on VCRs.

Candid angle lens Lens attachment that has a 45° mirror built in, so that you can record subjects at 90° to the direction you are facing. Useful for recording candid shots of subjects, as they are less aware of the camera.

CCD (charge-coupled device) The image-recording chip inside the camcorder on which the light falls. The CCD converts light to electrical signals that are recorded on to the tape.

Chrominance The colour component of the signal. In hi-band camcorders (Hi8, Super VHS and S-VHS-C), the video signal is split into luminance (brightness) and chrominance (colour). Processing the two signals separately helps improve the picture quality and avoid effects such as moiré patterning – the wave-like interference seen on fine patterns in a scene.

Colour correction Control found on most processors that allows you to vary the relative strengths of the red, green and blue parts of the signal. Enables you to correct incorrect colour balance or tweak the signal.

Colour temperature Measure of the colour composition of light, measured in Kelvin. The higher the colour temperature, the bluer the light. Ranges from red (2,000K) through indoor tungsten bulbs (around 3,400K), white daylight (5,600K), fluorescent (around 6,500K) to deep blue skies (up to 10,000K).

Composite video Combination of chrominance and luminance signals, which are processed together in lo-band (8mm, VHS-C, VHS) camcorders. Using this system, as opposed to the hi-band component video system (where the two signals are split) reduces both the cost of equipment and the quality of the signal.

Control-L (LANC) Edit control socket found on many 8mm and Hi8 camcorders. With the appropriate lead, information about the camcorder's tape counter position can be transmitted to a video recorder (for synchro-edit) or edit controller. Tape transport commands (play, record etc) can also be sent along the lead so that the camcorder can be recorded by remote control.

Control track Series of electronic identification pulses laid on a videotape to help guide the camcorder's video heads and keep them correctly aligned.

Conversion factor Amount by which a lens converter modifies the focal length of a lens. A 2x converter doubles the focal length of the lens.

Cue-review Tape transport function that gives fast playback either forward (cue) or reverse (review). Allows easy location of desired edit point.

Cut The edit point between two shots where one shot ends at full intensity, and the next begins at full intensity. Cut occurs every time you pause the tape.

Cutting rate How long the shots in a scene last on-screen. If most of the shots are short, the scene has a fast cutting rate. If most are lengthy, the cutting rate is slow. If most shots are of a similar length, the cutting rate is regular.

Day for night Technique where a blue filter is placed over the lens and the scene is underexposed to give the appearance of a moonlit night when the shot is recorded during the day.

Daylight preset Manual override of the camcorder's automatic white-balance system that is matched to daylight colour temperature. Preset should be used where camcorder might be confused – for instance when recording a warm sunset or fireworks, where the camcorder might set a

tungsten setting instead. Setting a tungsten setting in these circumstances would boost the blues and wash out the colours.

Depth of field The distance between the nearest and farthest points in a scene that are in focus. There is a greater distance behind the point of focus that is sharp than in front of it. Depth of field increases: the wider the lens setting used, the further away the point of focus and the narrower the iris.

Dew If camcorder heads get damp, tapes can stick to them, causing damage. Camcorders have built-in dew detectors that flash in the viewfinder. When dew is detected, the camcorder will not record or playback. Normally only a problem in very humid countries.

Diffuser Any substance that diverts some of the light rays falling on it, so that harsh lights are softened. Used over video lamps, the lighting looks far less intrusive. Dedicated diffusion material can be bought from professional photographic shops.

Digital frame store Camcorder facility that stores either the dark or light areas of a scene and superimposes the image over live video. Used mainly for storing titles, but can be used for matte effects – for instance to give the impression the shot is recorded through a keyhole.

Digital video (DVC) Video recording system set to supersede analogue formats (such as 8mm and S-VHS). The principle advantage of digital over analogue is that the quality of the video is not degraded by copying. Cassettes are smaller than 8mm or VHS-C too.

Digital zoom Lens that zooms into telephoto by electronically enlarging the centre of the image, rather than shifting glass elements inside the lens. This makes it possible for camcorders to be smaller and have longer zoom ranges, but quality is reduced the greater the degree of magnification.

Dioptre adjustment Means of adjusting a viewfinder to compensate for difference in a viewer's eyesight.

Dissolve (mix or cross-fade) Decreasing the intensity of one shot while increasing the intensity of another. For a short time both shots appear on screen simultaneously.

Dolly Any platform on wheels on which the camcorder operator or a camcorder tripod can be placed. Dedicated tripod dollies are available, consisting of three castors attached to a metal frame that connects to the bottom of the tripod.

Dynamic microphone Microphone that can generate a signal without the help of a battery.

Edit VCR Video recorder with features that make editing easy – specifically, front-mounted A/V sockets and a jog/shuttle. Hi-band format (Hi8 or S-VHS), insert edit and audio dub are also useful.

Electret microphone Common battery-operated microphone. Electret microphones are fitted to camcorders.

Exposure system Circuitry in a camcorder that measures the light level in a scene and sets the appropriate iris setting to expose the subject correctly. A subject is correctly exposed when the greatest amount of detail is retained.

Sometimes the camcorder can expose for the wrong part of the scene, rather than the required subject, and in these circumstances it is best to switch to manual exposure.

Fade Decreasing the intensity of the sound and video signal until the screen is black and the sound records nothing. Some camcorders increase the intensity of the video signal when the fade button is pressed, so the screen is rendered white. You can also fade into a scene.

Field Individual snapshots recorded by the camcorder. Either 50 or 60 are recorded each second, depending on the TV standard being used.

Fish-eye lens Ultra-wide-angle converter placed over the lens to give a panoramic but distorted view of a scene.

Fluorescent preset Manual white balance preset used when recording fluorescent lighting. When the fluorescent light cannot be seen by the camcorder (for instance when the camcorder measures colour temperature through the lens and no light is in shot), it might assume it is recording in a green environment, such as a forest, and set daylight balance. This would result in a very green image.

Flying erase head Video head drums contain an erase head that erases everything from the tape before recording a new signal. During insert edit this is not required, so a flying erase head is also included that wipes the video and hi-fi stereo sound only, leaving the control track and linear mono audio track untouched. Without flying erase heads, clean inserts would not be possible.

Format Type of cassette used by a camcorder. There are six domestic analogue formats: 8mm, VHS-C, VHS, Hi8, S-VHS, S-VHS-C and one domestic digital format: DVC.

Frame A single image, comprising two fields interlaced together. Either 25 or 30 are recorded per second, depending on the TV standard in operation.

Frequency response Range of sound frequencies that can be recorded by a camcorder's sound system. Low-frequency sounds include bass drums and rumbling thunder, whereas high-frequency sounds include whistles and screams.

Gain The amount of amplification given to a signal. When gain is increased on a camcorder, a greater current is supplied to the CCD making it more sensitive to light. There is also a loss in picture quality, however.

Genlock Device that synchronizes two signals so that there is no picture disturbance when they are displayed on screen together. Essential in vision mixers and when mixing live video with computer-generated titles and images.

Graphic equaliser Piece of hardware that can boost or reduce selected frequencies in an audio signal. Useful in reducing high-frequency hiss without affecting rest of signal.

HDTV (High-definition television) TV system that offers considerable advances in picture quality over PAL, SECAM or NTSC.

Head drum Rotating drum in camcorder or VCR on which recording and playback heads are situated. VHS linear mono head is fixed, and not located on the head drum.

Hi-band The better quality analogue formats (namely Hi8, S-VHS and S-VHS-C)

Hi8 Hi-band version of 8mm.

In-camera editing Determining shot order and duration at time of recording. Difficult to judge everything correctly, but has the advantage that no post-production is involved.

Inner focus (internal focus) Lens design that enables production of smaller lenses and thus smaller camcorders. The disadvantage is the sacrifice of manual zoom levers. Many models also sacrifice convenient manual focusing ring for inconvenient +/– buttons.

Insert edit Clean insertion of a new piece of video (and sometimes hi-fi stereo audio) without erasing mono audio or control track or causing any picture break-up at beginning or end of inserted shot.

Iris Adjustable opening between the camcorder's lens and CCD. The opening made by the iris is called the aperture. The greater the aperture, the more light that passes through the iris. The size of the aperture is measured in f-stops. The smaller the f-number, the greater the aperture. So f/1.4 would be very wide, whereas f/22 is very narrow. A stop is a doubling or halving of the amount of light entering the iris. An aperture of f/16 lets in twice the amount of light as f/22, and so is said to be one stop difference. Each of the following numbers is one stop smaller than the previous: f/1, f/1.4, f/2, f/2.8. f/4, f/5.6, f/8, f/11, f16, f/22, f/32. Only a handful of camcorders display the iris setting they are working at.

Jog/shuttle Circular control dial found on some VCRs and edit controllers that allows you to find edit points quickly and accurately by moving the tape forward or backwards very slowly, very quickly or frame by frame.

Kelvin Measure of colour temperature. The higher the colour temperature in Kelvin, the bluer the scene.

Linear edge track Mono audio track found on VHS camcorders and VCRs. Suffer from hiss and has low-frequency response, but can be rerecorded independently from other signals if camcorder or VCR features audio dub.

Lithium ion batteries Type of camcorder battery that doesn't suffer memory effect, as NiCad batteries do.

Lo-band Standard camcorder formats, namely VHS, VHS-C and 8mm.

LTC (linear or longitudinal time code) Alternative time-code method to RCTC and VITC used by some computer editing packages. Time-code information is recorded on linear edge track, so mono audio is lost.

Luminance The brightness component of a video signal. Processed separately from chrominance (colour) signal on hi-band camcorders, but together with chrominance signal on lo-band recordings.

Lux level Measure of the intensity of light. Camcorders can record in very low lux levels, but to achieve a reasonable exposure, they have to boost the gain, causing the image to look grainy and to lose contrast.

Macro Technically, any shot where the subject is reproduced life-size on the CCD, but also used to mean any close-up video or photography. Most camcorders can focus in macro as close as a few millimetres from the front of the lens. Depth of field is very narrow when you focus this close.

MEC (master edit control) Synchro-edit system used by and exclusive to JVC.

Memory effect Loss of running time afforded by NiCad batteries when battery is not disharged before recharging. Topping up the battery in this way can gradually reduce running time till only a few minutes is offered. Fully discharging and recharging the battery a number of times can eliminate memory effect.

Multistandard VCR Video recorder capable of playing back tapes recorded in a different TV standard.

NiCad (nickel cadmium) battery Most batteries used by camcorders are NiCads. A NiCad battery should last for around 1000 recharges.

NTSC (National Television Systems Committee) Television standard used in Japan and much of the Americas.

Pace Measure of the speed the action progresses in a movie. Pace is mainly determined by the action in a shot, but short-duration shots and an irregular cutting rate can increase the pace, whereas long shots and a regular cutting rhythm can slow it down. Pace is also slowed by transitions such as dissolves and fades between shots.

PAL (phase alternating line) Colour TV standard used in much of Europe, Australia, East Africa, India and China.

PCM (pulse code modulation) Hi-fi audio system found on some top-end Hi8 camcorder and VCRs.

Phono plug/socket Connection used for both video and audio. Sometimes referred to as an RCA connector.

Pixels (picture elements) Small colour-imaging elements on an LCD screen or a CCD.

Processor Device for improving picture during its transfer on to a copy tape. Brightness, colour and contrast signals can be enhanced during transfer, and some processors also give access to special effects.

Program modes Method of exposure control found on some camcorders, where you select the type of scene you want to record, and the camcorder selects the right iris setting, shutter speed and gain to achieve the best results. So, for instance, select portrait mode, and the camcorder sets a wide iris to throw the background out of focus. Select twilight, and the camcorder doesn't boost the gain to increase the light level.

RCTC (rewritable consumer time-code) Method of labelling every frame so that RCTC-equipped edit controllers can edit shots with extreme accuracy. Exclusive to 8mm and Hi8 camcorders.

RGB (red, green, blue) Method of splitting the video signal into separate

red, green and blue components – very little quality is lost using this method.

SCART 21-pin plug for connecting audio and video signals between video recorders and TVs, or between two VCRs. Also known as Euroconnector and Peritel.

SECAM (*sequencial couleur à memoire*) Colour TV standard used in France, the ex-Soviet Union, the Middle East and West Africa.

Shutter speed The length of time a charge is supplied to the CCD to enable it to record a single field. Standard shutter speeds are $\frac{1}{50}$th sec (SECAM/PAL) and $\frac{1}{60}$th sec (NTSC). Higher shutter speeds can be selected, and these freeze movement in the frame so that action can be analysed frame by frame or in slow motion. When played back at normal speed, moving subjects recorded with fast shutters such as $\frac{1}{1,000}$th sec appear to move very jerkily. This is known as strobing. Some camcorders allow slower shutters to be selected. These record fewer fields per second, and should be used for lowlight scenes without movement.

S-RGB converter Device that connects between a hi-band camcorder or VCR and a colour TV monitor that has standard SCART that is not wired for S-video. The S-signal is converted to RGB, and the maximum picture quality is retained.

Steadicam JR A support that uses carefully balanced weights and counter-weights to keep the camcorder level when you use it to record while walking. Because it has no contact with the ground, it can be used in rugged terrain.

Still video Still photography format that stores images electronically (the light is registered on a CCD, like in a camcorder). The still image is then downloaded on to a rerecordable floppy disk. Video outputs allow the image to be transferred directly to tape.

Synchro-edit Simple editing system that relies on a control lead between camcorder and VCR, so that both machines can be controlled by one set of buttons. Pre-roll delay is also built into the synchro-edit system, to compensate for backspacing. Compatible hardware has to be used, as there are several different systems available.

TBC (time-base corrector) Device that generates new control pulses to replace degraded originals. One of the results of this is that vertical lines in the frame become more clearly defined.

Transition One of the various ways of ending one shot and starting another. The most basic is the cut – when one shot ends at full intensity and the next starts immediately at full intensity. Others include fades, dissolves and wipes.

Trick play Playing back the tape at any speed or direction other than at normal forward play speed.

Tungsten preset Manual white balance preset to match the average colour temperature of interior lights (such as household bulbs). In practice, colour temperature of artificial lights can vary greatly.

TV standards Television system used by TV, camcorder or VCR. Although there are one or two hybrid systems

(principally in South America), most countries use either PAL, SECAM or NTSC.

Vision mixer Device that can take two or more separate video inputs and display them both on-screen at the same time. Useful for wipes and dissolves.

VITC (vertical integrated time-code) VHS time-code system. Video frames are individually labelled for frame-accurate editing. VITC cannot be added to a tape without disturbing other signals, so it has to be added either at time of recording or when copying from one tape to another.

White balance System used in camcorders that measures the colour temperature of the scene and sets the appropriate colour biases to record an accurate signal, where white subjects in the scene are rendered pure white. Some camcorders offer manual override and presets for different conditions.

White-balance lock A fully manual white-balance system where the camcorder is pointed at a piece of white card. The white-balance system measures the colour temperature of the light being reflected from it and uses this as a reference from which to determine correct colour balance.

Wide shot Composition that shows the whole subject, rather than a close-up detail. Useful for introducing a scene, but if the whole scene is recorded in wide shot, the viewer can feel distanced from the action.

Wildtrack Ambient sound recorded at a location and dubbed on to a video recorder at the editing stage.

Index